Hugh

God Only Knows

AMBER LANE PRESS

All rights whatsoever in this play are strictly reserved and application for professional performance should be made before rehearsals begin to:
Judy Daish Associates Ltd,
2 St Charles Place,
London W10 6EG

Application for amateur performance should be made before rehearsals begin to:
Samuel French Ltd,
52 Fitzroy Street,
London W1P 6JR

No performance may be given unless a licence has been obtained.

First published in 2001 by
Amber Lane Press Ltd,
Church Street, Charlbury, Oxford OX7 3PR
Telephone: 01608 810024

Printed and bound by
The Guernsey Press Co Ltd, Guernsey, C.I.

ISBN 1 872868 30 4

CHARACTERS

VIN COKER
KATE, his wife
CHARLES MINTO
ELEANOR, his wife
HUMPHREY BIDDULPH

A farmhouse in Tuscany. The present.

I am indebted to all the friends who helped and encouraged me during the writing of this play, particularly Clement Freud, Simon Gray, Anthony Page and Christopher Stace. I owe a very special debt to my wife, Rohan McCullough, and to my son, Tom Whitemore.

God Only Knows was written with Derek Jacobi in mind. He was wonderfully generous with his time and creative energies, providing me with many stimulating ideas and (often) trenchant criticism. Without him, the play would not exist and it is therefore dedicated to him with gratitude and affection.

Hugh Whitemore
February 2001

God Only Knows was first presented by Duncan C. Weldon for Triumph Entertainment Limited at the Malvern Festival Theatre on 31 August 2000 and subsequently at the Vaudeville Theatre, London on 20 March 2001. It was directed by Anthony Page with the following cast:

HUMPHREY BIDDULPH	Derek Jacobi
VIN COKER	Richard O'Callaghan
CHARLES MINTO	David Yelland
KATE COKER	Margot Leicester
ELEANOR MINTO	Francesca Hunt

Designer	John Gunter
Lighting Designer	Chris Davey (Malvern)
	Peter Mumford (London)
Sound Designer	John Leonard

ACT ONE

The shrill chirping of cicadas.

A pool of light amidst darkness.

Four people are sitting around a table, playing a game with dice and cards. They are wearing casual summer clothes. KATE. VIN *and* CHARLES *are in their fifties;* ELEANOR *is a little younger.*

For a few moments they play in silence. The smoke from CHARLES' *cigar coils up into the evening air. The atmosphere is tense, creating the impression that these people are possibly hardened gamblers in the middle of a crucial game. This impression does not last long.*

Vin throws the dice.

VIN   God! – look at that.

            [KATE *laughs.*]

        [*to* CHARLES] How much?

CHARLES   Thirteen thousand.

VIN   Thirteen...?

CHARLES   'Fraid so.

VIN   It can't be.

CHARLES   Well, it is.

VIN   *È ridicolo.*

KATE   Pay him, Vin.

VIN   Why does this always happen to me?

CHARLES   Happens to us all, old cock.

KATE   Pay him, Vin – get on with the game.

           [*Paper money changes hands.*]

CHARLES　*Grazie.*

VIN　*Prego.* I'll tell you a story.

ELEANOR　Once upon a time.

VIN　Once upon a time – not so long ago – two American mathematicians thought they'd found a way to beat the market.

ELEANOR　To do what...?

VIN　Beat the stock market.

ELEANOR　How?

VIN　By devising a formula to eliminate risk.

CHARLES　I've heard about this.

[KATE *is holding the dice.*]

KATE　Whose go is it?

VIN　Brilliant mathematicians. They won the Nobel Prize.

CHARLES　The hedge fund people.

VIN　Correct.

ELEANOR　How is it possible to eliminate risk?

VIN　By hedging your bets. You bet the market will move in one direction and hedge out the risks by betting in the opposite direction.

ELEANOR　Is this a true story?

VIN　Absolutely. They believed they could make unimaginable sums of money. Profit without risk. The holy grail.

KATE　Why are you telling us this?

VIN　Because I always lose at Monopoly.

ELEANOR　You don't.

VIN　Always. And I thought of those two young mathematicians. Perhaps they could invent a formula to help me win.

CHARLES Drop them a line.

VIN I might.

>[KATE *is still holding the dice.*]

KATE Whose go is it?

CHARLES Yours.

KATE I'm still in jail.

ELEANOR Must be mine. [*to* VIN] So what happened?

VIN They raised three billion dollars and started to invest. Everyone thought they were on to a winner – and for a time, it looked as if they were.

>[ELEANOR *throws the dice.*]

ELEANOR Eight. *Via Accademia.* Who's got the *Via Accademia?*

CHARLES Nobody; it's still for sale.

ELEANOR How much?

CHARLES Fourteen thousand – cheap at the price.

>[ELEANOR *and* CHARLES *exchange 'Monopoli' money and property cards.*]

VIN Trouble was, hedge funds operate in some strange sort of financial cyberspace – interest rate swaps, currency derivatives, repurchase agreements. Nobody understood what was going on. They had to take it on trust. Very dodgy.

CHARLES You're the sort of chap who likes to keep his money in a sock under the bed.

VIN Well at least I know where it is.

>[CHARLES *throws the dice.*]

CHARLES Seven. *Corso Magellano.* Mine.

VIN It's like all these dot com companies.

KATE What is?

VIN Everything's based on expectation. Nobody gives a toss about financial realities. All mindless optimism.

[CHARLES *gives the dice to* VIN.]

CHARLES It's called greed. Getting something for nothing.

VIN Not just greed. People love the possibility that the impossible is about to become possible. It's profoundly comforting. We want to believe that all natural laws will be turned upside down and it'll be profit and happiness for ever and ever, amen. [*He throws the dice.*] Three. *Viale Costantino.* Right, that's me finished.

CHARLES Yes, well – *Viale Costantino* with three houses – eighty thousand, I'm afraid.

VIN Eighty thousand! You'll be lucky. All I've got is twenty-two, twenty-three, twenty-four – twenty-eight thousand. *Niente*, skinto.

ELEANOR You could mortgage the Water Works.

VIN What's the point? Charles is bound to win.

CHARLES Not necessarily.

VIN You're bound to.

CHARLES Not necessarily. Look at yesterday: all those houses on the *Via Roma* – I lost the lot.

[KATE *stands up.*]

VIN You won in the end, though. You always win. I always lose. [*to* KATE] Where are you going?

[KATE *exits into the house.*]

CHARLES You give up too easily.

VIN I give up when I'm bored.

CHARLES And sod the rest of us. Charming.

[*An off-stage light is switched on (by* KATE) *and the location is revealed: a paved terrace outside*

> *a converted farmhouse in Tuscany. Night. Summer. Light floods onto the terrace from the house and from an external lamp above the door. The trees and shrubs beyond are shrouded in darkness.*]

VIN   Don't be so touchy – the game's over – you've won.

CHARLES   Stick to the rules. Finish the game.

VIN   You've won, I've lost, Kate's buggered off and your nice new wife couldn't give a damn either way.

ELEANOR   I was enjoying it.

VIN   Where's the wine?

CHARLES   Over there. Look, there's no point in playing if you don't stick to the rules.

VIN   Sticking to the rules is a thing of the past. Like boy scouts, suspender belts and newsreaders with posh accents.

> [*He picks up the half-empty bottle of red wine and offers it to* ELEANOR.]

Vino?

ELEANOR   Please.

CHARLES   Bloody anarchist.

VIN   Up yours. [*calling*] Bring another bottle of red!

> [*He refills* ELEANOR's *glass and then his own.* CHARLES *is making a desultory attempt to tidy the table.*]

ELEANOR   What are you doing?

CHARLES   Clearing up.

ELEANOR   Not yet, please.

> [CHARLES *obeys.*]

I want to know what happened to the Americans and their magic formula.

VIN   Ah well. Disaster.

       [*He gives* ELEANOR *her glass of wine.*]

ELEANOR   Thanks.

VIN   They lost a trillion dollars.

ELEANOR   How much...?

VIN   A million million.

ELEANOR   God.

VIN   I find it rather heart-warming. The magic formula was not, as they thought, all-powerful. In 1997 the Asian markets collapsed; a few months later Russia refused to pay its international debts. Mathematical logic could not foresee either event. A victory for the unpredictable. A triumph for human imperfection. I like that.

CHARLES   How do you know all this?

VIN   Research. I thought I might write a thriller about a nerdish Ph.D. who works for the Chase Manhattan.

CHARLES   You could call it "Fear at the FTSE".

VIN   "Death on the Dax".

CHARLES   "Horror at the Hang Seng".

       [*They laugh.* KATE *returns, carrying a bottle of San Pellegrino.*]

KATE   The phone's still not working.

CHARLES   It was the storm.

VIN   Does it matter? Where's the wine?

KATE   What wine?

VIN   I asked you to bring another bottle.

CHARLES   [*to* KATE] Don't worry about the phone. We'll drive into town and have a few sharp words with those layabouts in the estate office.

VIN   That won't do much good. They'll just stare at us with undisguised contempt and mutter anglophobically amongst themselves.

KATE   Make a fuss! Tell them it's important. I hate not having the phone.

ELEANOR   So do I.

VIN   We'll see about it tomorrow.

KATE   You said that yesterday.

[VIN *stands up.*]

VIN   I'll get some wine.

KATE   I do wish you wouldn't drink so much.

VIN   [*to* CHARLES] She thinks I'm drunk.

CHARLES   And so you are.

VIN   On this stuff? Do me a favour.

[*He goes towards the house.*]

ELEANOR   Don't go, Vin. Finish the story. What happened to the mathematicians?

VIN   Ah, well. The American government bailed them out.

ELEANOR   Why?

VIN   Losses on that scale would've destroyed confidence in the entire system. Global collapse. The punters would've lost faith. All the markets would've crashed.

[*There is a terrible noise in the darkness: the splintering metallic thump of a car crash.*]

CHARLES   What was that?

KATE   It sounded like a crash.

VIN   A crash...?

ELEANOR   It can't have been.

VIN   A car crash...?

CHARLES   It sounded bad.

ELEANOR   It can't have been a car crash.

CHARLES   Why not?

ELEANOR   Cars don't come along here.

> [*Pause. Nobody moves.*]

KATE   What shall we do?

CHARLES   Perhaps we ought to go and have a look.

VIN   It's the middle of the night.

KATE   Half past ten.

VIN   Eleanor's right. Nobody drives along that road after dark.

KATE   We'd better go and look.

VIN   All of us...?

CHARLES   You and Kate stay here. We'll go.

ELEANOR   We'll need a torch.

KATE   I think we should all go.

VIN   No point in everyone going.

ELEANOR   Where's the torch?

KATE   In the kitchen –

CHARLES   I'll get it.

KATE   – by the fridge.

> [CHARLES *hurries to the house.*]

VIN   Look, I think we should wait a bit –

ELEANOR   For what?

VIN   There's bugger-all we can do, chasing around in the dark.

ELEANOR   We've got to do something.

> [ELEANOR *goes to the house.* KATE *makes a move to follow.*]

KATE   I think we should go with you.

> [CHARLES *appears briefly at the french window;*
> *he is carrying a torch.*]

CHARLES   Stay here. I'll yell if we need help.

ELEANOR   [*off*] Come on!

> [CHARLES *follows* ELEANOR. *Pause.* KATE *glares*
> *at* VIN.]

KATE   Why do you always do this?

VIN   Do what?

KATE   You let Charles do everything.

VIN   Do what?

KATE   Everything.

VIN   For God's sake...!

KATE   Why didn't you go with him? Why didn't you offer to help?

VIN   He told us to stay here!

KATE   Oh Vin.

VIN   Oh Vin what?

KATE   We should've gone with them.

VIN   I don't know what you're talking about.

KATE   Yes you do.

VIN   Charles does not do everything. Who went to the supermarket yesterday?

KATE   If Charles hadn't made all the arrangements, we wouldn't be here. I kept asking you to ring the travel agent. You did nothing.

VIN   I did nothing because I didn't want to come. Why are we here? Charles isn't my friend. Pompous prat.

KATE   He's our friend and I'm very fond of him.

VIN   He was our friend when he was married to Alice. I thought Alice was your great chum. Why are we still friends with Charles and not with Alice?

KATE   We are still friends with Alice. I am, anyway.

VIN   We never see her.

KATE   Stop arguing, Vin – and don't have another row with Charles. Please don't spoil the holiday.

VIN   Spoil the holiday...? God Almighty, there's not much to spoil. Three weeks in an overpriced barn with rotten plumbing, dodgy electrics and no telephone. Lousy pool. Miles from anywhere. Nothing but paperbacks by Danielle Steel and Jeffrey Archer. Terrific.

[He goes to the house.]

KATE   Where are you going?

VIN   To get some more wine.

[He exits.]

KATE   No, Vin, please – we don't need any more...

[She follows him into the house.]

[Pause.]

[There is a movement amongst the shadows. A man appears in the darkness just beyond the terrace. It is HUMPHREY BIDDULPH. *He stands very still and alert, like a hunted animal, watching, listening.]*

[He steps forward into the light. He is in his fifties, wearing pyjamas, bedroom slippers, and a lightweight bomber jacket (several sizes too large for him) with Rolling Stones World Tour *printed on the back. He is holding a revolver. He walks cautiously across the terrace. Seeing that there is no immediate danger, he puts the revolver in his jacket pocket.]*

[KATE *comes out of the house. She sees* HUMPHREY *and screams.* VIN *is immediately behind her, holding a bottle of red wine. Seeing* HUMPHREY, *he grasps the bottle like a club.*]

VIN Who the hell are you?

HUMPHREY You're English!

[*He sinks onto a chair and weeps.* KATE *and* VIN *stare in amazement.*]

KATE What is it? Are you hurt?

HUMPHREY I can't tell you how wonderful it is to hear an English voice.

[KATE *and* VIN *stand side by side, wondering what they should do.* HUMPHREY *gradually regains his composure.*]

I'm sorry. There's been an accident.

VIN Your car...

HUMPHREY Straight into a tree.

KATE Are you all right?

HUMPHREY I think so.

VIN You're bleeding.

HUMPHREY Am I? Where?

VIN Your head.

[*There is a graze on* HUMPHREY's *forehead; he dabs at it with his fingers.*]

HUMPHREY Nothing, it's nothing.

KATE We heard this dreadful noise. We thought it was a crash.

VIN We weren't sure.

KATE The others have gone to have a look.

HUMPHREY [*suddenly alert*] What others...?

KATE Our friends.

HUMPHREY Oh I see. Your friends. Are they English or Italian?

KATE English.

HUMPHREY I can't believe you're all English! Perhaps my luck's beginning to change.

VIN What about you? Are you alone?

[HUMPHREY *is momentarily puzzled.*]

HUMPHREY Alone?

VIN Was anyone travelling with you?

HUMPHREY Oh no. No, I am alone.

KATE What happened?

HUMPHREY Lapse of concentration, I suppose. I've been driving such a long time. You know how it is. The road suddenly got very narrow – or seemed to.

KATE It's only a farm track.

HUMPHREY Is it? I see. A farm track. Yes, that would explain a lot. I thought I saw a man standing directly in front of me. Arms outstretched. I swerved to avoid him. Crashed into a tree.

KATE Who was it?

HUMPHREY I don't know. It must've been a trick of the light. When I got out of the car – nobody there.

VIN Probably one of the poachers.

HUMPHREY One of the what?

VIN Poachers. We hear them every night. Hunting the wild boar.

[KATE *is unconvinced by this.*]

KATE They never come anywhere near the house.

VIN We don't *know* that. We just haven't seen them.

HUMPHREY Where exactly am I?

KATE The nearest town is Montivellara.

HUMPHREY Is that on the road to Florence?

VIN Good Lord, no.

KATE You should be on the A1.

HUMPHREY I thought I was.

KATE That's much further east.

[ELEANOR *enters breathlessly.*]

ELEANOR It's really strange – there's a car but nobody in it.

VIN He's here.

[*He gestures to* HUMPHREY.]

ELEANOR I don't believe it! Is that his car?

HUMPHREY It is.

ELEANOR You're English!

HUMPHREY I am.

ELEANOR I don't believe it. [*calling to* CHARLES] He's here! He's all right! [*to* HUMPHREY] What happened?

HUMPHREY I went into a tree.

ELEANOR There's a lot of damage.

HUMPHREY I know.

[CHARLES *enters and stares at* HUMPHREY.]

CHARLES Good God Almighty.

ELEANOR [*to* HUMPHREY] We thought you must be dead. [*to* CHARLES] He's English.

HUMPHREY I was extremely lucky.

CHARLES Are you all right?

HUMPHREY I appear to be.

CHARLES The car's a write-off. What happened?

HUMPHREY I can't remember much about it.

CHARLES We thought you'd gone through the windscreen. There's glass all over the place.

[*He bends forward to look at* HUMPHREY's *forehead.*]

You're bleeding.

HUMPHREY It's nothing – just a graze.

ELEANOR Would you like a drink?

KATE Tea – isn't that what they give people after an accident? Strong sweet tea.

CHARLES That's right.

HUMPHREY Actually, I'm not a great tea drinker, actually.

VIN Brandy? Glass of wine? Fizzy water?

HUMPHREY Water would be nice. Thank you.

[VIN *pours water into a glass.*]

ELEANOR Where were you going?

HUMPHREY North.

VIN Firenze.

CHARLES You should be on the A1.

KATE He thought he was.

CHARLES No, no, that's miles away.

[HUMPHREY *takes the glass of water from* VIN.]

HUMPHREY Thank you.

[ELEANOR *looks at* HUMPHREY's *face.*]

ELEANOR That's more than just a graze.

HUMPHREY Nothing to worry about. I'm perfectly all right.

CHARLES Perhaps we should get you to a hospital.

HUMPHREY No, no –

CHARLES   Or at least find a doctor.

HUMPHREY   No, please –

CHARLES   There must be a doctor around here somewhere.

HUMPHREY   No, please – absolutely no need.

ELEANOR   Delayed shock can be very nasty.

KATE   We can drive into Montivellara. It won't take long.

CHARLES   Good idea. You'll have to report the accident anyway.

HUMPHREY   Leave it, please leave it.

CHARLES   Is it a hired car?

HUMPHREY   Leave all that to me.

CHARLES   I think you ought to tell the police.

[HUMPHREY's *response is surprisingly impassioned.*]

HUMPHREY   No, please – I beg you – leave all that to me! Please! [*He appears to regret this outburst; he continues more calmly.*] Let me just sit quietly for a minute. Let me collect my thoughts.

[*A moment of silence; they look at him with varying degrees of puzzlement.*]

I think perhaps I would like a drop of wine – if that's possible...

VIN   Of course.

[VIN *pours wine into a glass.*]

CHARLES   What's your name?

HUMPHREY   My name...?

CHARLES   Your name.

[HUMPHREY *does not respond immediately.*]

That thing people call you when they want to attract your attention.

HUMPHREY Oh, my name. Ha. Yes. Biddulph. Humphrey
Biddulph.

CHARLES Charles Minto –

[HUMPHREY *takes the glass of wine from* VIN.]

HUMPHREY Thank you.

CHARLES – my wife, Eleanor. Kate and Vin Coker.

KATE Hullo.

ELEANOR Hullo.

HUMPHREY You must forgive my appearance. I wasn't expecting – as it were – to meet people.

CHARLES Where have you come from?

[HUMPHREY *fails to answer this question, perhaps deliberately.*]

HUMPHREY Living alone, you see, that's the reason. One tends
to neglect the orthodoxy of everyday life – wearing
conventional clothes, for example, when the neces-
sity to do so is not immediately apparent. Do forgive
me. [*raising his glass*] Salute. [*He drinks.*] This is very
good. Barolo?

VIN Gattinara.

HUMPHREY Ah yes, I thought it was *Piemontese*. [*He sips his wine;
he sees the 'Monopoli' board on the table.*] You've been
playing Monopoly.

ELEANOR In Italian.

HUMPHREY How delightful. So – you're here on holiday?

ELEANOR Yes.

HUMPHREY Very nice. Charming villa.

KATE Are you on holiday, Mr Biddulph?

HUMPHREY On my way to meet a friend.

KATE In Florence?

HUMPHREY　Venice.

KATE　You're driving all the way to Venice?

HUMPHREY　Well, yes. At least, I was – before I hit the tree.

ELEANOR　What are you going to do now?

HUMPHREY　I'm not entirely sure. Not. Entirely. Sure.

KATE　You must stay here.

CHARLES　[*displeased*] Here...?

KATE　Just for tonight. We can get things sorted out in the morning.

HUMPHREY　Oh no, I can't do that. I mean – [*a nervous glance at the dark landscape*] – just in case – I mean – I couldn't possibly...

KATE　Why not?

ELEANOR　If only the phone was working.

HUMPHREY　What's wrong with it?

VIN　There was a storm a couple of nights ago. Hasn't worked since.

HUMPHREY　Don't you have a mobile?

ELEANOR　We didn't bring it.

CHARLES　We don't want phone calls on holiday.

ELEANOR　*You* don't.

HUMPHREY　What about your neighbours? Perhaps their phone is working.

ELEANOR　There's no one. Just an old farmer about a half a mile away.

VIN　Surly sod.

ELEANOR　He won't talk to us.

HUMPHREY　I see. [*Brief pause; he takes a sip of wine.*] Well in that case...

KATE　Yes?

HUMPHREY If it's not too much of an imposition – I would be glad
          of a rest – a couple of hours, say – on the sofa...

CHARLES   If you're staying, you'd better stay the night. Tomor-
          row morning we'll take you in to Montivellara.

HUMPHREY Whatever you say.

CHARLES   [*to* VIN] That's the best thing, don't you think? He
          can see a doctor. Hire a car. Inform the police.

HUMPHREY Thank you.

    VIN   Fine by me.

   KATE   Would you like something to eat?

HUMPHREY Oh no. Thank you.

   KATE   There's salad in the fridge. Prosciutto.

ELEANOR   Salami and cheese.

HUMPHREY No, no, you mustn't go to all that trouble.

ELEANOR   It's no trouble.

   KATE   Stay here, it won't take a minute...

          [*She heads for the house.*]

HUMPHREY Please let me help...

          [HUMPHREY *stands up, but he loses balance and
          lurches unsteadily towards* CHARLES.]

    VIN   Catch him, quick, catch him!

          [CHARLES *manages to guide* HUMPHREY's *fall-
          ing body into a chair.*]

HUMPHREY I'm so sorry – terribly sorry –

          [*He slumps, panting, into the chair.*]

   KATE   Are you all right?

HUMPHREY Suddenly felt giddy.

ELEANOR   Shock.

CHARLES   Yes.

HUMPHREY It was the wine –

ELEANOR Delayed shock.

HUMPHREY – I haven't had a drink for several weeks.

CHARLES We'll get you to a hospital.

HUMPHREY No, no –

KATE You must see a doctor.

HUMPHREY No, please!

CHARLES You must. No arguments.

> [HUMPHREY *responds with a shout of anguish.*]

HUMPHREY I can't! I can't!

> [*Silence. They all look at him with alarm.* CHARLES *takes control.*]

CHARLES Look – you've had a bad accident. You're in shock. You may've injured yourself –

HUMPHREY You don't understand...

CHARLES – and since you've come here, to our house, it's our responsibility to make sure you get proper medical treatment.

HUMPHREY If I go to hospital, if I see a doctor, it all becomes official – I can't risk that.

ELEANOR Risk what?

CHARLES Go and get the car, Vin.

HUMPHREY No! Please! Stop!

ELEANOR Risk what?

HUMPHREY Please, I beg you.

ELEANOR Are you in some sort of trouble?

HUMPHREY No. Well, yes – but not in the way you mean.

CHARLES What way is that?

HUMPHREY I haven't done anything wrong.

VIN   What have you done?

HUMPHREY   Nothing. I have done nothing.

VIN   So what are you afraid of?

[HUMPHREY *hesitates for a moment.*]

HUMPHREY   There are people looking for me.

VIN   People?

HUMPHREY   I think.

VIN   What people?

HUMPHREY   From the clinic.

CHARLES   What clinic?

HUMPHREY   I really can't explain.

VIN   Why not?

HUMPHREY   It's just too complicated.

VIN   What is?

ELEANOR   I think we should go to the police.

CHARLES   I think so too.

HUMPHREY   No, please – please don't – please!

ELEANOR   We don't know who you are, we don't know where you've come from, we don't know what you've done.

HUMPHREY   I am not a criminal. I am not a dangerous man.

CHARLES   In that case, tell us what's going on –

HUMPHREY   I can't!

CHARLES   – if you've got nothing to hide, tell us. Otherwise, we go to the police.

[*Silence.*]

HUMPHREY   It's something I know. Something I've found out. There are people who want to silence me.

KATE   Who?

VIN   Found out what?

HUMPHREY Don't ask. It's better you don't know.

VIN What d'you mean?

HUMPHREY Safer. Less risky.

VIN Safer...?

CHARLES You say you've done nothing wrong. How can we be sure of that?

HUMPHREY Can't you take it on trust?

CHARLES Would you?

[HUMPHREY *sighs.*]

HUMPHREY No. Probably not.

ELEANOR The point is – we know nothing about you.

KATE Nothing.

HUMPHREY Well fine, that makes us quits.

KATE What do you mean?

HUMPHREY I know nothing about you.

VIN Charles is an architect. He builds houses in Egham and Camberley for young men in suits and their socially climbing wives. Eleanor has a fabric and interior design business. Wife number two. I write mediocre scripts for third-rate television series. In more ambitious days I met Kate, who was secretary to the deputy Head of Drama at the BBC. Her best friend was Alice, secretary to the Head of Light Entertainment. Alice was married to Charles. We all became friends. Every year we holiday together. Sometimes in Spain, sometimes in France, sometimes in Italy. What more can I tell you?

[*A long silence.*]

HUMPHREY Forgive me. Where would I find the, uh...?

CHARLES I'll show you.

HUMPHREY   Forgive me...

KATE   Put some disinfectant on that cut. There's a bottle on the bathroom shelf.

HUMPHREY   I will. Thank you.

[CHARLES *leads* HUMPHREY *into the house. A moment of silence.*]

ELEANOR   Amazing.

VIN   Bizarre.

ELEANOR   I need a drink.

[*She pours herself a glass of wine.*]

KATE   What do you make of him?

ELEANOR   Weird.

VIN   Extremely.

ELEANOR   He's wearing pyjamas.

VIN   And bedroom slippers.

KATE   He explained that. He said he wasn't expecting to see anyone.

VIN   You don't drive all the way from wherever to Venice wearing pyjamas and bedroom slippers.

ELEANOR   And that jacket. I mean – really weird.

KATE   He's just a bit eccentric.

VIN   Perhaps he's escaped from the local loony bin.

KATE   What would a middle-aged Englishman be doing in an Italian loony bin?

VIN   You tell me.

ELEANOR   What do you think we should do?

VIN   I don't know.

KATE   He's obviously frightened. I think we should help him.

ELEANOR   How?

KATE Let him stay overnight. That's no great problem, is it?

VIN I think we should get him to a hotel.

KATE What hotel?

VIN There are dozens in Montivellara.

KATE It's August, Vin, they'll be full up.

VIN We can try, can't we?

KATE It's almost eleven.

VIN So?

KATE It'll be midnight by the time we get him to a hotel. They'll all be in bed.

VIN We can wake them up.

[CHARLES *returns*.]

KATE Is he all right?

CHARLES Seems to be.

ELEANOR You shouldn't have left him alone.

CHARLES I can't go to the lavatory with him.

ELEANOR What happens if he's taken ill?

CHARLES He's all right. Just a bit shaken up.

VIN Perhaps we should have a look in his car.

KATE Why?

VIN To see if there are any clues.

ELEANOR Clues...?

VIN To confirm or support his story.

ELEANOR Don't you believe him?

VIN Do you?

KATE I think we should give him the benefit of the doubt.

VIN Why?

KATE Why not?

VIN He's escaped from somewhere and he's on the run.

CHARLES Why do you think he's escaped from somewhere?

VIN Pyjamas and slippers. Doesn't that suggest a hurried departure?

CHARLES Perhaps he's ill. He said he was in a clinic.

ELEANOR God – perhaps he's got some dreadful disease.

VIN Like what?

ELEANOR I don't know. Something awful.

KATE He doesn't look ill.

VIN There must be something wrong with him, otherwise he wouldn't be in a clinic.

CHARLES All the more reason to get him to a doctor.

ELEANOR Where's the nearest hospital?

VIN Miles away.

> [HUMPHREY *appears at the french windows. He has cleaned the graze on his forehead.*]

KATE How are you feeling?

HUMPHREY I think perhaps I should go.

KATE Go...?

HUMPHREY Leave. Be on my way.

VIN You can't do that.

HUMPHREY Why not?

VIN No car.

HUMPHREY I can walk.

VIN All the way to Montivellara?

HUMPHREY Is it far?

VIN Twenty kilometres.

HUMPHREY Perhaps I could ask you for a lift...

CHARLES If we take you to Montivellara, we take you to the police.

HUMPHREY Trust me. Please.

CHARLES We could land ourselves in real trouble. I'm not prepared to take the risk.

HUMPHREY Please. Don't do this. I beg you.

CHARLES Don't do what?

HUMPHREY Don't get involved. It'll only make things worse.

CHARLES We *are* involved. You crashed your car outside our house. Sooner or later somebody's going to come asking questions. We need to know the answers.

> [HUMPHREY *sinks onto a chair and buries his face in his hands.*]

HUMPHREY Why did this have to happen – *why?* [*He raises his head and looks at them.*] I don't know what to do. I am a law-abiding citizen. You must believe that. I'm a solitary, rather reclusive person. An academic, for Christ's sake. A scholar. That's why I came here in the first place.

VIN To do what?

HUMPHREY I was offered a job.

KATE In Italy?

HUMPHREY In Rome. I knew it'd be a mistake. But I was flattered. Stupid, stupid, stupid! I should never have come here. [*He sees a glass of wine on the table.*] Is that mine?

VIN Yes. What sort of a job?

HUMPHREY I'm an expert in old documents. Incunabula.

ELEANOR Incunabula...?

HUMPHREY Early printing.

CHARLES What's so flattering about working in Rome?

HUMPHREY Not just Rome. The Vatican. They could choose anyone. Anyone in the world! They chose me. And I'm
not even a Christian.

VIN To do what?

HUMPHREY I've been sorting through a collection of documents
known as the *Archivio Segreto.*

VIN The Secret Archive.

HUMPHREY Yes, but it's not really secret – that's what they call
it. Hundreds of thousands of documents and letters,
going right back to the Middle Ages – earlier. Someone had the bright idea of publishing facsimiles of
the more interesting items – Henry VIII's letters about
his divorce, for example – publishing them in book
form, a limited edition, the highest quality – and
I was hired as adviser and editor and to provide
whatever historical or explanatory notes they deemed
necessary.

[*Silence.*]

VIN Well go on. Tell us what happened.

[HUMPHREY *hesitates. Another long, tense
silence.*]

HUMPHREY Are any of you Roman Catholics?

VIN No. [*to* ELEANOR] You're not, are you?

ELEANOR No.

KATE Why do you ask?

HUMPHREY I don't want to make the same mistake twice.

KATE What mistake?

HUMPHREY Like telling Father Henriques.

ELEANOR Telling who?

HUMPHREY I might find myself in even deeper trouble.

ELEANOR Who's Father Henriques?

HUMPHREY It's because of him I'm in Rome. I knew him in the old days. It was through him I got the job.

VIN And he's the one who's landed you in all this trouble?

HUMPHREY Well, yes. Well, no. I can't explain.

VIN Try.

[HUMPHREY *is again engulfed by fear.*]

HUMPHREY Please try to understand. I've just been through the most extraordinary and alarming weeks of my life. I don't know what to do.

KATE Look, we want to help you. But Charles is right. You've got to tell us what it's all about. Is that so very unreasonable?

[*There is a momentary silence before* HUMPHREY *speaks.*]

HUMPHREY You may find it rather disturbing.

KATE In what way?

VIN Get on with it.

HUMPHREY I'm just warning you.

VIN All right. We have been warned.

[HUMPHREY *drinks his wine in a single gulp.*]

HUMPHREY There was this man. Rinato Morandi. He rang up and asked me to his house. I had no idea who he was or what he was. Complete stranger. I suppose I should never have gone. No! – wait. Before that. At the embassy. I met him at a party. Drinks at the embassy. I have a friend who works there. That's where I met him. Four or five weeks ago. Rinato Morandi.

CHARLES This is in Rome...?

HUMPHREY Yes. I live there – I've lived there almost six years.

ELEANOR And you met this man at the British Embassy in Rome...?

HUMPHREY Yes. He was charming, very friendly. I was grateful for that. I'm not too good at official functions. It was a relief to have a proper conversation with someone. It was only later I realised how strange it was.

VIN Strange...?

HUMPHREY He knew so much about me. He knew I worked at the Vatican. He knew about my interest in ancient documents. And he asked so many questions.

VIN Like what?

HUMPHREY How long had I worked in the Secret Archive? Do I have any connection with the Roman Catholic hierarchy? Why was I, a non-Catholic, chosen for this particular job?

CHARLES Why were you?

HUMPHREY Ah well, you know the Catholics – always a pragmatic breed. My expertise outweighed my ungodliness.

KATE Wasn't it difficult for you – being a non-believer?

HUMPHREY Not really. The *monsignori* endured my scepticism – a patronising smile on their lips. They were, of course, convinced it masked a repressed or rejected faith. Arrogant buggers.

> [*This shaft of antagonism creates a brief tremor of surprise.*]

ELEANOR Go on about Mr Morandi.

HUMPHREY He said how delighted he was to meet me and he really seemed to mean it. He made me feel rather special, rather glowy, which doesn't happen very often, not to me, anyway – and because of this, I dropped my guard somewhat. Big mistake. He asked for my phone number and left. I never expected to see him again.

To my great surprise, he rang the following morning – very early – and asked me for a drink that evening. Actually he asked me for a cocktail. Rather quaintly old-fashioned, I thought. "Do come for a cocktail." I was astonished. And enormously intrigued.

ELEANOR   I bet.

HUMPHREY   He lived in one of those large sombre villas near the *Via Appia Antiqua* – huge overgrown garden – umbrella pines – security gates – surly, beady-eyed servant. Very Henry Jamesian – the servant, not the security gates. The house was full of antique statuary, some of it very fine. Morandi told me he was a dealer. He talked quite openly about his work. He was remarkably frank – one might say, foolishly indiscreet. He made it perfectly clear that some of his activities were far from being strictly legal. In Italy there are very precise regulations governing the private sale of national antiquities. Morandi obviously paid scant attention to these bureaucratic restrictions. He told me he supplied "special" pieces – special meaning illegal – to rich collectors.

CHARLES   You mean he's a crook...?

HUMPHREY   Well, yes – up to a point.

CHARLES   Up to a point...?

HUMPHREY   To be honest, I didn't really take any of that on board. I found it all rather exciting. Nothing like this had ever happened to me before. [*another stab of self-recrimination*] But you're right. It's all my own stupid fault. God, I was such a fool..

[VIN *offers the comforting bottle of Gattinara.*]

VIN   Have some more wine.

HUMPHREY Thank you.

[VIN *refills* HUMPHREY's *glass.*]

He took me up to his study – it was on the first floor – a most attractive room, lined with books and sales catalogues. There was a large window overlooking the garden. The pool, I noticed, was empty, with a scattering of pine needles in the bottom. Morandi opened the safe and took out a box file. Inside was a photocopy of an ancient document and certificates of authentication relating to the carbon dating of the original document. He told me to take it away (the photocopy), to prepare a rough translation (it was in Latin) and give an opinion as to its textual authenticity. For this relatively undemanding task, he offered me the sum of fifty thousand US dollars. Cor blimey, guv'nor, you could've knocked me dahn with a feather. He also told me to keep the whole thing strictly confidential. If only I had. I put the documents into my briefcase. We returned to the *salone*, drank another bloody Mary and discussed AC Milan's three-goal victory over Fiorentina. The surly servant doubled as chauffeur. He drove me home. Before I had a chance to examine the document – the telephone. My sister from Australia. Most distressing. Her marriage was on the rocks, poor thing, floods of tears. I was dreadfully upset – forgot all about Morandi's document, had several large brandies, and went to bed. Woke late. No time for breakfast. Went to work. It is, as you can imagine, the most extraordinary experience to spend one's working life in the Vatican. Very different from catching the Central Line to Bond Street. To stroll across the *Piazza San Pietro*, walk along Bernini's colonnade, through the great bronze doors, the *Portone di Bronzo* – and then to follow the Swiss Guard along the *Scala Reggia*. All carefully designed, I'm sure, to create a profound sense of awe and majesty and patriarchal power. It certainly succeeds in doing so. [*losing himself for a moment*] Where was I?

VIN   Going to work.

HUMPHREY   Ah yes. By this time, of course, I'd completely forgotten about the papers in my briefcase and it wasn't until I'd had several large espressos that my head began to clear and I remembered the events of the previous evening. I opened my briefcase and read the document. It was – well, astonishing. I can safely say it was the most astonishing moment in the whole of my life – certainly the whole of my professional life. It was then that I made my big mistake. I decided to show the document to Father Henriques.

KATE   This is the man who got you the job at the Vatican?

HUMPHREY   Yes. He'd been a history don at Oxford before he entered the Church. That's when I met him. Wonderfully knowledgeable, I'd have been lost without him. We spent many hours together, arguing furiously about our beliefs and non-beliefs. "Humphrey the heathen," he used to call me. I regarded him as my good friend and wanted to share my excitement with him – but in my impulsive haste, I forgot he's now first and foremost a devout Roman Catholic priest. Does what he's told. Catholics – as you may or may not know – have no right to question let alone dissent from the literal truth of all papally defined dogma. Dissent is, in fact, a sin. I went to his office and gave him the document. He read it quickly (his Latin is far better than mine) and said "Fuck!" under his breath. He asked me where it came from, and I gave him a brief account of my meeting with Mr Morandi. "I think I should show this to Monsignor Casement," he said – no question of "May I?", "Is it all right?", he just put the paper into his pocket and left.

VIN Who's Monsignor Casement?

HUMPHREY One of the top bananas. Member of a Vatican tribunal known as the Congregation for the Doctrine of the Faith. Before 1965, it was called the Holy Office. Before 1542, it was called the Holy Inquisition. Its function, now as then, is to enforce an inflexible observance of all Catholic doctrine – the Immaculate Conception, the Resurrection, papal infallibility, the Assumption of the Virgin Mary, the whole caboodle. And like the Inquisition, it operates in total secrecy. It was the Inquisition, you'll remember, who accused Galileo of heresy when he said the earth went round the sun. He was told he'd be put to death pronto if he didn't change his mind and recant – which of course he did, poor old sod, who can blame him? As Camus once said, the truth isn't worth that degree of sacrifice. He was killed in a car crash, did you know that? *Carbonisé*, as they say so vividly in the French newspapers. I thought of him. funnily enough, as my car hit the tree.

[ELEANOR *is becoming increasingly confused.*]

ELEANOR Galileo was killed in a car crash...?

VIN Albert Camus.

HUMPHREY January 4th, 1960. Only forty-six. He was driving from Provence to Paris. Before he left, he wrote post-cards to his wife and three of his mistresses. "Longing to see you" – same message to all of them. By the time they received their postcards, he was dead. Since

I heard that story, I've been very careful about what and to whom I write before setting off on a journey.

CHARLES   So you gave this document to Father Henriques and he gave it to Monsignor what's-his-name.

HUMPHREY   Casement. Correct.

ELEANOR   What happened then?

HUMPHREY   I went back to my office. Not feeling too good. Actually rather ropey. Bloody Marys and cheap Spanish brandy is not a clever combination. [*He stops suddenly.*] I shouldn't be telling you this.

KATE   Why not?

HUMPHREY   It's all too vague.

KATE   What is?

HUMPHREY   I can't remember exactly what happened. Everything seems blurred and out of focus. Probably because of the drugs.

CHARLES   Drugs...?

HUMPHREY   Perhaps I closed my eyes, perhaps I dozed a little. I seem to remember the door opening. Somebody in the room. Then – momentary images – faces, voices – I seemed to be slipping in and out of consciousness, not at all an unpleasant sensation, rather the reverse, very restful and comforting. Then I woke up – fully alert, with a remarkably clear head. I was in a strange place. In bed, in my own Marks and Spencer pyjamas. Bare white walls. A trolley with a bedpan and medical paraphernalia. I was in a hospital! – but where and why? I decided to investigate. I struggled out of bed – legs a bit woozy – found some slippers (my own slippers!) and made my way across to the door. Suddenly there was the most almighty clattering of bells – clearly I had set off some sort of alarm system.

The door was thrown open by a gigantic young man. The Incredible Hulk in all but name. He manhandled me back into bed, by which time a white-haired *dottore* had appeared on the scene. He told me I had suffered a mild, but significant, heart attack. Complete rest was essential, he said, and for that reason, I would be sedated for the next few days. When I asked where I was, how long I would be kept there, how I could contact family and friends, he told me not to worry – everything would be taken care of. I was given an injection and fell asleep. During my brief spells of consciousness, I observed that the windows were barred. I was guarded night and day by the Incredible Hulk or somebody equally Hulkish. I was a prisoner. I tried to complain. Futile. Nobody listened. They held me down and gave me more injections. I had terrible fits of uncontrollable rage. It was a nightmare. Then – one day last week, can't remember when exactly, I seem to have lost all sense of time – Father Henriques came to see me. I was furious – demanded explanations, demanded freedom, etcetera. He deliberately ignored me – kept asking questions about Morandi's document. I couldn't believe this man was one of my closest friends. He seemed utterly changed. We ended up shouting – screaming – at each other. It was very alarming. He stormed out and slammed a newspaper down onto the bedside chair. *La Repubblica.* On page three there was an item about a car crash on the auto-strada south of Turin. The driver had been killed instantly. He was described as a dealer in antiquities. His name was Rinato Morandi.

VIN   God.

HUMPHREY It was obviously intended as some sort of none-too-subtle warning. Keep quiet or else.

KATE You mean – you mean you think they killed Mr Morandi because of the document he showed you?

HUMPHREY I do, yes.

CHARLES Probably just another accident. Plenty on the autostradas, after all.

KATE It might've been another man called Morandi.

HUMPHREY There was a photograph.

[*There is a brief silence while everyone considers this information.*]

ELEANOR Where is this place?

HUMPHREY What place?

ELEANOR The clinic. Where you've been.

HUMPHREY Somewhere near Rome, just off the A12.

KATE Perhaps you did have a heart attack.

HUMPHREY Most unlikely.

CHARLES Why?

HUMPHREY For one thing, they didn't exactly treat me like a patient. Quite the reverse. And for another, I had a check-up a couple of months ago. My doctor said my heart was in remarkably good nick.

KATE So what do you think happened?

HUMPHREY I think somebody came into the office while I was half asleep and rendered me unconscious.

CHARLES How?

HUMPHREY Injection, perhaps.

[*This is too much for* CHARLES.]

CHARLES Oh come on!

ELEANOR   Wouldn't you have felt something?

HUMPHREY Not if he or she were skilled in such matters.

VIN   And then whisked you off to this clinic?

HUMPHREY That is my theory, yes.

CHARLES   All because of the document you got from Mr
Morandi?

HUMPHREY Yes.

KATE   Why? What's in the document?

[HUMPHREY *is astonished.*]

HUMPHREY What's in the...? Didn't I tell you?

KATE   No.

HUMPHREY Ha! Well – be glad. Be grateful.

[*The sound of distant gunshots.* HUMPHREY
swings round in alarm.]

What's that?

VIN   Poachers.

HUMPHREY What?

VIN   Poachers. We told you.

HUMPHREY Oh yes. Poachers. Hunting the wild boar. Yes, you
said. [*He takes a gulp of wine. Pause.*] Perhaps. On
second thoughts. Perhaps I shouldn't tell you any
more about this wretched document.

KATE   Why not?

[*Another gunshot. A dog is barking.*]

HUMPHREY Are you sure they're poachers?

VIN   We hear them every night. Regular as clockwork.

KATE   Why shouldn't you tell us about the document?

HUMPHREY Dangerous knowledge, Mrs Coker. At least you can tell
them – quite truthfully – you know nothing about it.

KATE   Tell them...? Tell who?

HUMPHREY   The people who are looking for me.

KATE   You mean – [*She looks anxiously at the shadow-filled garden.*] – you mean, you think they may've followed you here...?

HUMPHREY   It's possible.

ELEANOR   How could they possibly know where you're going?

HUMPHREY   I needed petrol. I stopped at a garage about thirty kilometres away. A blaze of neon light. Everything else in darkness. There were two men on duty. I paid with a credit card I found in this jacket. Not mine, needless to say, I pinched it from the clinic. They stared at the credit card. They whispered something. One of them went into the office and made a quick phone call. He came back, gave me a charming smile, and returned the credit card. I went back to my car. On the forecourt, there was a white Fiat Punto. A man was sitting inside. Watching me. As I drove away, I saw him making a call on his mobile phone.

VIN   Might've been ringing his girlfriend.

HUMPHREY   I think not. They knew I had no money. They knew I'd be forced to use the Visa card – they knew they could trace it.

KATE   They...?

HUMPHREY   The people at the clinic.

ELEANOR   How could they trace it?

HUMPHREY   Everything's computerised these days. And this is Italy, don't forget – the Vatican has eyes everywhere.

CHARLES   Now look – you'd better tell us – exactly and precisely – what this is all about. What is this document?

HUMPHREY   It's better you don't know. Believe me.

ELEANOR   If you've landed us in some sort of danger the least you can do is to tell us about it.

VIN   That's right. She's right. You've got to tell us.

CHARLES   If not, we go to the police. Simple as that.

> [*Pause. The dog is still barking.* HUMPHREY *looks at* CHARLES. *He speaks a Latin phrase that was the customary greeting at the beginning of many Roman letters.*]

HUMPHREY   *Marcus Sempronius Quinto suo salutem plurimam. Si tu vales ego valeo.* It's a letter – a letter written by a Roman senator to a close friend (the tone is unusually racy and informal). Date, around one hundred, one twenty, AD (or CE as we now have to call it, CE for Common Era – hideous, don't you think? – reeking of political correctness). Marcus Sempronius, the letter writer, and his family had just recovered from a mysterious illness which he blamed on one of the house-slaves – a man suspected of being a Christian. Marcus couldn't take Christianity seriously, as he explains in his letter. His grandfather, Lucius Sempronius, had been a military intelligence officer in the Roman garrison in Jerusalem when Pontius Pilate was governor. It seems life was not easy for the Romans – they were undermanned, for a start, and Palestine was a difficult province to govern. Social stability was constantly being threatened by the emergence of various rabble-rousers: prophets, miracle-workers, would-be messiahs, all of whom attracted little bands of disciples and followers. Reports about these various sects were sent to the grandfather, Lucius, who had to decide whether or not they posed any sort of security threat. One of these reports concerned a Jewish magician and healer called Yeshua ben Pantera, or Jesus the Nazarene, known as Chrestus or Christ, the Anointed One. His following, although modest, was on the increase, so Lucius read the report with more than usual care. However, it turned out that Yeshua preached love and forgiveness – he was clearly a good man – but what intrigued Lucius most particularly was the phrase "Love Your Enemies", which seemed to be a unique feature of Yeshua's teaching. Lucius realised that if more and more Jews could be persuaded to Love Their Enemies, the Romans' task in Palestine would be made substantially easier. He spoke to Pilate, suggesting that they should encourage more Jews to join the cult that was growing up around Yeshua. The question was – how? The answer, they decided, was to fabricate or manufacture a resurrection – resurrection myths were very popular in those days – the idea of a life after death was especially potent in a society where most people could look forward to nothing but grinding poverty, incurable disease and painful death. Lucius and Pilate contrived to make the myth a reality, to give the people what they yearned for. Proof. Certainty. The unfortunate Nazarene was arrested on the trumped-up charge of calling himself King of the Jews. With a little help from the Jewish priests (who were only too happy to put the boot in), he was found guilty and crucified. Normally it was the custom of the Romans to leave the corpse hanging on the cross until it was eaten by birds. Not this time. Lucius gave permission for Yeshua's body to be laid in a tomb belonging to one of his disciples – a rich man called Joseph of Arimathea. Thus the stage was set for a resurrection. The body was smuggled out of the tomb – they found a Galilean who looked

not unlike the dead man and bribed him to imper-
sonate the risen Christ – bit of a gamble – and as
we know from the New Testament, people didn't
recognise him at first, they thought he was an angel
or a gardener or a stranger on the road to Emmaus.
But because they were so eager to believe, they were
all eventually convinced. Even Mary. The writer ends
his letter by reflecting how surprised his grandfather
would be if he could see how rapidly the cult has
grown over the past hundred years. Before very long,
he opines, Jesus the Nazarene will be worshipped as
widely as Jupiter or Mars.

[*A moment of astonished silence.*]

VIN Unbelievable!

HUMPHREY So you can see why Father Henriques said "fuck".

ELEANOR Do you think it's real?

HUMPHREY Real...? How do you mean?

ELEANOR Do you believe it's true?

HUMPHREY You mean is the document genuine? Impossible to
say. I examined it for – what? – a couple of hours,
no more, and it was only a photocopy. The carbon
dating certificates seemed authentic enough.

KATE Where did it come from?

HUMPHREY It was part of a job lot. A dealer had died and his effects
were being sold off.

KATE Before that. Where's it been for the last two thousand
years?

HUMPHREY These things do turn up from time to time.

KATE Do they?

HUMPHREY Oh yes.

KATE Not things like this, surely?

HUMPHREY Oh yes, absolutely. Look at the Dead Sea Scrolls.

VIN What about them?

HUMPHREY They just turned up. Nobody knew they existed. An Arab shepherd boy found them in a cave near the Dead Sea. Thirteen papyrus books hidden in an earthenware jar. He thought they might fetch a few bob in the local market. He took them home. His mother used some of them to light the fire. The boy took them to a local sheik. The sheik sold them to a Christian shopkeeper in Bethlehem. He sold them to a Syrian priest. He showed them to a scholar at the Hebrew University. And so they went from hand to hand, from expert to expert, until they ended up in Baltimore of all places, at the Johns Hopkins University, where a professor described them as "the greatest manuscript discovery of modern times". And they just turned up – out of the blue.

ELEANOR So you think Mr Morandi's document is genuine?

HUMPHREY It might be. It could be. One can't ignore the possibility.

VIN Seems more than a possibility to me.

CHARLES Why?

VIN If these people didn't think it was genuine, they wouldn't be chasing him halfway across Italy.

KATE We don't know for sure they are chasing him.

VIN They locked him up in the clinic.

CHARLES "They"...? Who are "they"?

VIN The Vatican, presumably. Father Henriques and his chums.

ELEANOR Why should the Vatican be so concerned? Surely they could just ignore it – say it's all nonsense.

HUMPHREY "If Christ be not risen, then our faith is in vain."

CHARLES Who said that?

KATE St Paul, I think – didn't he?

HUMPHREY I believe he did.

CHARLES Kate, I'm very impressed.

VIN My wife is a secret churchgoer – didn't you know that?

ELEANOR In other words, without the resurrection, Christianity wouldn't exist.

HUMPHREY Exactly. Precisely.

VIN Ha! I'm not surprised the Vatican's worried.

ELEANOR Oh come on, this one document's not going to undermine the whole of Christianity.

VIN It might.

ELEANOR Vin, be sensible.

VIN Anything's possible.

HUMPHREY Gods are not immortal, Mrs Minto.

CHARLES [*dismissively*] Oh really!

> [HUMPHREY *ignores this. He continues to address* ELEANOR.]

HUMPHREY Look at Odin and Thor, Aphrodite, Ra and Osiris. People worshipped them with the same fervour and conviction that Christians worship Jesus Christ. Now they're all dead. Extinct, like the dinosaurs. [*He displays his empty glass.*] May I?

> [VIN *gestures assent.*]

Thank you.

> [*He pours himself some wine.*]

KATE Did you realise what it meant? – when you first read the letter – did you realise the implications?

HUMPHREY Yes, I think so.

KATE Weren't you frightened.?

HUMPHREY Exhilarated. First exhilarated, then frightened. [*He takes a sip of wine.*] When I was a child there was a picture above my bed, one of those sentimental prints showing Gentle Jesus, meek and mild, surrounded by an adoring assembly of fluffy animals and curly-headed Aryan toddlers. As I read Morandi's document that picture flashed into my mind. I hadn't thought of it for over forty years. And there I was, holding in my hand a piece of paper that could dump the whole fraudulent charade into the trash-can of human gullibility. My mouth went dry. I could hardly breathe.

KATE Perhaps you should've pretended the letter was a fake.

HUMPHREY Oh I couldn't. Why do that?

CHARLES Couldn't...? Why not?

HUMPHREY I suppose – well I suppose because I think the truth shouldn't be concealed, no matter where it may lead or what it may do.

KATE Is it the truth?

HUMPHREY What do you think?

CHARLES Can you prove any of this, Mr Biddulph?

HUMPHREY Do please call me Humphrey. Ridiculous name, I know – my mother was halfway through *Humphrey Clinker* when I was born – God knows why she was wasting her time with Smollett, I find him totally unreadable. [*replying to* CHARLES] Can I prove any of this? Well no, not a word.

VIN So why should we believe you?

HUMPHREY Why should I choose to invent such a farfetched and extravagant story?

CHARLES Who else have you told?

HUMPHREY Nobody. Apart from Father Henriques, of course. The *dottore* at the clinic asked me a few questions, medical questions, nothing about Morandi.

VIN Did they threaten you? – the people at the clinic?

CHARLES Did they tell you what they were going to do?

HUMPHREY No. I got the impression they were waiting.

CHARLES For what?

HUMPHREY I don't know. Orders, perhaps.

CHARLES From whom?

HUMPHREY I don't know.

VIN And you escaped when? – this morning?

HUMPHREY Lunchtime.

ELEANOR How long were you there?

HUMPHREY About – I don't know – three weeks at least.

KATE How did you get out?

HUMPHREY The water heating system went wrong – it's always going wrong – there's no hot water when you want to shave or have a bath – but when it's midday and the sun is blazing, click! the radiators turn themselves on, and you're dying of heat. That's what happened this morning. I made urgent and repeated complaints – an engineer was called and started to examine the water pipes in my room. Because of the intense heat, he removed his bomber jacket; he is – as you see – [*displaying the excessive length of his jacket sleeves*] – somewhat bigger than me. Having diagnosed the problem, he left the room to turn off the mains water. He forgot to lock the door. I picked up his jacket –

this jacket. His car keys were in the pocket. I couldn't believe it. I got the hell out, ran for my life and found his car.

CHARLES How?

HUMPHREY The car keys were for a Renault. Only one Renault in the carpark.

KATE And nobody stopped you...?

HUMPHREY Nobody seemed to notice. It was lunchtime. The place was deserted.

ELEANOR Where was the Incredible Hulk?

HUMPHREY Absent. Presumably he thought the engineer would be keeping an eye on me.

CHARLES Luckily for you.

HUMPHREY Very lucky. So off I went – top speed, like the clappers. Petrol tank almost full. Incredible.

CHARLES Almost too good to be true.

HUMPHREY Trouble was: no maps in the car – finding my way to Venice was a major problem – and when it got dark, virtually impossible, which is why I got lost and crashed into your tree.

CHARLES Why didn't you go to the police?

HUMPHREY Why should I do that?

CHARLES If I'd been abducted and locked up it's the first thing I'd do.

HUMPHREY Can't trust the police. They're all in it together.

KATE All in what?

[HUMPHREY *ignores this.*]

HUMPHREY [*to* CHARLES] I think you're probably right: it *was* too good to be true. I think they wanted me to escape.

KATE Why should they?

HUMPHREY   After the row with Father Henriques they knew I wasn't going to play ball. If they wanted to get rid of me, they wouldn't do it in the clinic. Fouling your own nest. And the farther away from Rome the better.

CHARLES   Isn't this getting a bit fanciful? You don't *know* anyone's following you.

ELEANOR   What about those people he saw at the garage?

CHARLES   There could be a perfectly innocent explanation.

VIN   What so special about Venice? Why are you going there?

HUMPHREY   I have a friend. Bob. Bob Hobbes. Hobbes with an E. Writer. Perhaps you've heard of him. Wrote an excellent book about Frederick Rolfe, Baron Corvo. He has an apartment near the *San Marziale*. I shall be safe there. Fingers crossed, he'll get me a passport. Bob has friends who can provide almost anything.

ELEANOR   Where is your passport?

HUMPHREY   In my desk in my study in my apartment in Rome.

KATE   How are you going to get to Venice?

HUMPHREY   How am I going to get to Venice? [*This question seems not to have occurred to him. He frowns.*] Yes, that is rather a crucial question, isn't it? Dear-oh-dear.

CHARLES   Well, that's your problem, not ours. Thank God. [*He moves to the table.*] Come along. It's getting late. [*to* VIN] Give me a hand.

VIN   Every night we shift this sodding table into the house. Why?

CHARLES   It might rain.

VIN   It hasn't rained for the last ten days.

CHARLES   That doesn't mean it won't rain tonight.

VIN You like the routine, that's what it is. The bedtime ritual. Something to do with your potty training.

[VIN *picks up one end of the table and helps* CHARLES *carry it into the house.* KATE *is putting glasses and plates onto a tray.*]

KATE [*to* CHARLES] Perhaps you're jumping to the wrong conclusion.

CHARLES I don't think so.

KATE You might be. The people in the clinic couldn't possibly have known the central heating system was going to go wrong.

ELEANOR They might've fixed it.

KATE How?

ELEANOR By turning up the thermostat.

KATE The engineer would've seen that straight away.

ELEANOR Perhaps he was part of the plan. He left the door unlocked, after all.

KATE That's right, he did.

ELEANOR He left his bomber jacket behind, car keys in the pocket. All seems a bit suspicious to me.

[CHARLES *and* VIN *return.*]

CHARLES What does? What are you talking about?

ELEANOR The central heating engineer.

CHARLES Bugger the central heating engineer. [*turning crossly to* HUMPHREY] The sooner we get you out of this house, the happier I shall be.

HUMPHREY Actually, I've been thinking. One possibility does present itself.

CHARLES About what?

HUMPHREY My predicament.

KATE   What's that?

HUMPHREY   If you have no violent objections, I could take your car.

VIN   Our car...?

HUMPHREY   If I leave now I can drive through the night – presumably you have a road map – and phone the police anonymously to say that your car has been stolen.

[CHARLES *stares incredulously.*]

CHARLES   You're asking us to give you our car...?

HUMPHREY   It's not your car exactly, is it?

CHARLES   What do you mean?

HUMPHREY   I assumed it was rented.

VIN   Hang on a minute – hang on. You're seriously suggesting that you take our car and leave us here, stranded...?

HUMPHREY   Not stranded exactly.

VIN   No car, no phone – what else would you call it?

HUMPHREY   I'll call the police as soon as I get to Venice. They'll come to your rescue.

CHARLES   Out of the question.

HUMPHREY   You can say you never even saw me. Woke up in the morning and the car was gone.

CHARLES   Out of the question.

HUMPHREY   Please. There's no other solution.

VIN   You're not taking our sodding car.

HUMPHREY   It's not asking much, after all.

VIN   Not asking much!

HUMPHREY   A minimal inconvenience.

CHARLES   No – sorry – absolutely not.

[HUMPHREY *takes the gun from his jacket pocket.*]

HUMPHREY I'm afraid I must insist.

[*Everyone gasps.*]

I'm terribly sorry. Do forgive me.

ELEANOR Oh God.

[HUMPHREY *feels obliged to offer some explanation.*]

HUMPHREY It belongs to the central heating engineer – or so I suppose. I found it in his coat pocket. Obviously people who go to the clinic go armed.

KATE Please don't do this.

HUMPHREY I'm sorry, Mrs Coker.

CHARLES Give me the gun.

HUMPHREY I'll just take the car and leave.

CHARLES Give me the gun.

ELEANOR Don't argue with him, Charles.

HUMPHREY [*to* CHARLES] May I have the keys?

CHARLES The keys...?

ELEANOR The car keys.

CHARLES I haven't got them.

KATE Who used the car last?

ELEANOR Vin.

VIN Me? When?

ELEANOR When you went to the supermarket.

VIN They're on the hook by the kitchen door.

HUMPHREY Perhaps you could get them for me.

[VIN *makes a move towards the house.*]

CHARLES Don't do it, Vin.

VIN   What do you mean?

CHARLES   Call his bluff.

VIN   Call his bluff yourself.

> [*He goes to the house. He stares, astonished, at the hook by the door.*]

They're not here!

CHARLES   What?

VIN   The bloody keys.

HUMPHREY   I don't believe you, Mr Coker.

VIN   Look for yourself. They're not here!

HUMPHREY   I'll count to ten.

KATE   [*to* HUMPHREY] You mustn't, please...

HUMPHREY   One –

KATE   [*to* VIN] Where did you put them?

VIN   On the hook. I always put them on the hook.

HUMPHREY   Two –

KATE   [*to* HUMPHREY] Wait a minute. We'll go and look up-stairs.

ELEANOR   Why should they be upstairs?

VIN   Somebody must have taken them.

CHARLES   Don't start blaming me.

HUMPHREY   Three –

VIN   I wasn't blaming you.

ELEANOR   Don't argue, do something!

HUMPHREY   Four –

ELEANOR   For heaven's sake, do something!

HUMPHREY   Five –

> [*Blackout.*]

ACT TWO

Immediately following the end of Act One.

HUMPHREY Six –

KATE Please don't...

HUMPHREY Seven –

KATE Please...

HUMPHREY Eight –

KATE Oh please...

HUMPHREY Nine –

> [*Suddenly his whole demeanour changes. He stops counting and sinks onto a chair.*]

God, this is ridiculous – ridiculous! I'm sorry, I'm sorry – oh God.

> [*He offers the gun to* CHARLES.]

You'd better take this. I might set it off by mistake.

> [CHARLES *steps forward and takes the gun.*]

I can't believe I did such a thing – ludicrous! I've never held a gun before – total madness – panic, of course, that's what it was – suddenly overwhelmed by panic – self-preservation – nothing else matters. I'm so sorry.

> [KATE, ELEANOR *and* VIN *stand staring at him.* CHARLES *is examining the gun.*]

CHARLES It's not loaded.

VIN What?

CHARLES It's not loaded. [*to* HUMPHREY] Where are the bullets?

HUMPHREY I don't know.

CHARLES   Give them to me.

HUMPHREY   I haven't got any bullets. I told you. I don't know
           anything about guns.

CHARLES   Where did you get it?

HUMPHREY   I found it. In my pocket. I told you.

CHARLES   The pocket of that coat?

HUMPHREY   Yes.

CHARLES   Which you say belongs to the central heating engineer?

HUMPHREY   Yes.

CHARLES   Why should the central heating engineer – if there
           is such a person – why should he have a gun that
           isn't loaded?

HUMPHREY   I don't know.

CHARLES   Doesn't make sense.

HUMPHREY   I'm sorry.

CHARLES   Do stop saying that.

HUMPHREY   Well I am. Dreadfully sorry.

CHARLES   Go and get the car, Vin. We'll take him in to
           Montivellara.

    VIN   What, now...?

CHARLES   Of course now. You don't hang about when a man's
           just pointed a gun at you.

   KATE   It wasn't loaded.

CHARLES   So what? He didn't know that. [*to* VIN] Go and get
           the car.

    VIN   I can't.

CHARLES   Why not?

    VIN   The keys. We've lost the sodding keys.

CHARLES   Well find them! Do something useful for a change.

VIN I always put them on the hook. Someone must've taken them.

ELEANOR We must find them, Vin. We're completely stuck without the car.

VIN Don't panic. We'll ring Hertz and get them to send us another set.

KATE No phone.

VIN No phone. Shit.

KATE They must be around somewhere.

ELEANOR Try to remember what you did when you came back from the supermarket.

VIN Nothing. Just came back with the food.

ELEANOR Then what?

VIN Had a drink. Went for a swim. [*A sudden thought.*] Wait.

[*He runs to the door.*]

KATE Where are you going?

VIN Wait.

[*He goes into the house. The front door bangs open. A distant whoop of delight.* VIN *reappears at the door, triumphantly holding the car keys.*]

Eureka!

KATE Where were they?

VIN In the car.

CHARLES In the car...?

VIN So much bloody shopping – arms full, couldn't carry anything else – intended to go back for the keys – must've forgotten.

ELEANOR Thank God for that.

CHARLES Give them to me.

VIN Why?

CHARLES I'll drive. You've had too much to drink.

VIN Drive? Where are we going?

CHARLES Montivellara.

ELEANOR [*indicating* HUMPHREY] With him.

VIN Hang on a minute. We've got to talk about this.

CHARLES Talk about what?

VIN [*referring to* HUMPHREY.] Him. What's going to happen.

CHARLES There's nothing to talk about.

VIN I think there is.

CHARLES We're taking him to the police.

VIN I'm not sure whether we should.

CHARLES For God's sake...!

VIN It might be a mistake.

HUMPHREY A big mistake.

CHARLES Shut up.

KATE [*to* VIN] Why?

VIN Just suppose what he said is true. About being followed. We don't want to get mixed up in all that.

CHARLES All what?

VIN Whatever it is he's mixed up in. You heard what he said – they killed Mr Morandi.

CHARLES He said that to frighten us.

VIN Well he certainly frightened me.

ELEANOR And me.

CHARLES So what do you suggest?

VIN Perhaps his idea is best. Pretend he's stolen the car. Let him bugger off to Venice.

HUMPHREY Yes!

CHARLES What...!

VIN Why not?

HUMPHREY Yes, why not?

CHARLES Shut up. [*to* VIN] Don't be ridiculous.

ELEANOR Is it ridiculous?

CHARLES Of course it is.

ELEANOR Perhaps it isn't.

CHARLES For heaven's sake, Eleanor – we can't do that!

ELEANOR Vin's right. It might be true what Mr Biddulph says.

CHARLES I've never heard such an outlandish story – not a scrap of evidence to support it.

ELEANOR Maybe there is. That man he talked about – Mr Morandi – I'm sure I read about it. The car crash.

KATE Read about it where?

ELEANOR We bought a newspaper when we went to Siena.

VIN That's right, we did.

ELEANOR There was a dreadful photograph of a burnt-out car. [*to* CHARLES] Don't you remember? I showed it to you. Don't drive too fast on the way home, I said.

KATE We don't know it was Mr Morandi's car.

ELEANOR It could've been. It might've been.

VIN [*to* HUMPHREY] When did you first realise you were being followed?

HUMPHREY Early on. I wasn't sure. It was just a feeling.

CHARLES Paranoia.

VIN [*to* CHARLES] No, it makes total sense. They lock him up. He's on the run. They're bound to follow him.

KATE Or try to.

VIN Or try to.

ELEANOR Oh God, perhaps he's right. Perhaps they do want to get rid of him.

HUMPHREY Exactly!

KATE They wouldn't do that.

VIN Why not? He's the only person left alive who knows about the letter.

ELEANOR We know now. [*to* HUMPHREY] You told us.

HUMPHREY I did warn you.

VIN [*becoming alarmed*] This is serious.

HUMPHREY It is.

ELEANOR We ought to let him go, Charles.

CHARLES We can't.

VIN Why not?

CHARLES He's stolen a car. Comes here with a gun. We can't just let him go.

VIN Why not?

CHARLES We've got to protect ourselves, that's why. If he's involved with the Vatican, we've got to be bloody careful.

KATE Do stop being so melodramatic! It's only a letter. Nobody's going to get killed for a letter.

VIN They might – if it's important enough.

HUMPHREY That's right.

KATE You're all making too much of a fuss. If it's a fake they've got nothing to worry about, and if it's genuine – so what? It doesn't say Jesus Christ didn't exist. It says he did. The Vatican should be pleased.

HUMPHREY It may prove he existed – but only as a man – not the Son of God. That's a crucial distinction. If he's not the Son of God, if he didn't rise from the dead, Christianity has no validity. You said so yourself.

KATE   I can't believe this one letter's going to undermine the whole of Christianity.

HUMPHREY   It could do a lot of damage.

KATE   I can't see how.

HUMPHREY   Christianity's a great deal less substantial than most people believe. Rather flimsy, in fact.

KATE   What about Matthew, Mark, Luke and John? Why should we jump to the conclusion that they're wrong and this letter is right?

HUMPHREY   The gospels are notoriously unreliable.

ELEANOR   What do you mean?

HUMPHREY   As historical sources.

KATE   In what way?

HUMPHREY   Matthew, Mark, Luke and John aren't a history of actual events, more a collection of hand-me-down stories, hearsay myths, all strung together to form some sort of cohesive narrative – a PR job, if you like, designed to promote the new cult of Christianity which was being badly tarnished by nasty rumours of witchcraft and cannibalism.

ELEANOR   Cannibalism...?

HUMPHREY   "Take, eat – this is my body..."

KATE   You mean people thought...?

HUMPHREY   Well of course. Human sacrifice, the drinking of blood etcetera, was part of many ancient religions.

KATE   That's horrible.

CHARLES   So who actually wrote the gospels?

HUMPHREY   Nobody. I mean – no specific authors. The gospels were written and rewritten over and over again to make them fit in with existing myths and prophesies.

CHARLES   Like what?

HUMPHREY   Well – for example – Bethlehem. Jesus was a Nazarene so it's most unlikely he was born in Bethlehem.
Miles away. That was inserted into the gospels
because of an Old Testament prophesy – Book of
Micah, I think – "Out of Bethlehem shall come forth
a ruler in Israel." They were supposed to have gone
to Bethlehem because of a tax census. There was
no census at the time of Jesus' birth. There's no
historical corroboration for the Massacre of the
Innocents. The virginity of the Virgin Mary is a
mistranslation; in the original Hebrew the word
is "almah", which means a girl of marriageable age;
that became "virgin" when it was translated, or mis-
translated, into Greek. The assumed date of birth is
incorrect; it has to be 4 BCE or earlier, because King
Herod died in 4 BCE. And so on, and so on.

ELEANOR   You're saying it's all a fraud?

HUMPHREY   A fable. An elaboration.

KATE   Of what?

HUMPHREY   The most plausible theory I've come across suggests
that Jesus Christ was the illegitimate son of a Roman
soldier (Tiberius Julius Pantera). His mother was a
peasant woman called Mary whose husband was an
elderly carpenter. He, Jesus, was a charismatic
Galilean Hasid, probably married – not a Christian,
of course – Christ wasn't a Christian, he was Christ
– and he went from village to village, preaching and
healing the sick.

ELEANOR   So how do you explain that?

CHARLES   Explain what?

ELEANOR   The miracles.

HUMPHREY   Miracle-workers were a dime a dozen in ancient
Palestine. There were no hospitals, no insane

asylums, no drugs, scarcely any doctors. People were only too eager to believe that miracle-workers actually worked miracles. Therefore, ergo, there were bound to be a certain number of so-called miracle cures. Mind over matter. Happens all the time.

ELEANOR So Jesus – if he existed –

HUMPHREY Which he probably did.

ELEANOR – was just a wandering preacher, an itinerant faith-healer, one of many.

HUMPHREY One of very many.

KATE Why haven't the other faith-healers got their own religions? Where did Christianity come from?

HUMPHREY Ah well – Paul of Tarsus – moralising old bigot. He's the one who invented Christianity. He took the Jesus stories and wove them together with various pagan myths (Osiris, Dionysus, Mithras, particularly Mithras) and created a new cult based (as they all were) on the idea of death, rebirth and transformation.

ELEANOR Who's Mithras?

VIN Persian god.

HUMPHREY Born on the twenty-fifth of December, like somebody else we know. His followers practised baptism, believed that eternal life awaited the righteous, and whose most holy sacrament was a consecrated meal of bread and wine. Mithras sprang to life from a rock, and all temples dedicated to him were cave-like structures, carved in the shape of a rock. "Upon this rock I will build my Church." Makes you think.

VIN So the whole of western civilisation has been hood-winked and deceived – is that what you're saying?

HUMPHREY Of course that's not what I'm saying.

VIN   Sounds very like it to me.

HUMPHREY   I've read the books, that's all. I've studied the documents. Anyone could do it. You could.

CHARLES   Right, let's stop all this. We're not here to have a theological debate. We've got to decide what to do. If we're going to take him to Montivellara – which I certainly think we should – we ought to get a move on.

HUMPHREY   It's not a theological debate. I'm trying to explain why my life might be in very real danger.

KATE   Because of Mr Morandi's letter?

HUMPHREY   Because the origins of Christianity do not bear close examination. The more questions you ask, the more it unravels.

CHARLES   Be that as it may, it's getting late and we have to make some sort of a decision –

VIN   Hang on a minute, hang on. [to HUMPHREY] All this stuff you've been talking about – can any of it be proved?

HUMPHREY   That's the whole point, don't you see? – in these matters nothing but nothing is provable.

VIN   So it's basically what? – conjecture, guess-work, speculation?

HUMPHREY   Conjecture, but soundly based.

CHARLES   On what?

HUMPHREY   Historical investigations. Scholarly research. And the weight of informed opinion suggests – overwhelmingly – that the story of Christianity is far more fiction than fact.

KATE   So why has it survived? I mean if it's so flawed and full of holes, why has Christianity survived for two thousand years?

HUMPHREY Ah well – all sorts of reasons.

CHARLES Namely?

HUMPHREY In its early days, the Jesus cult had a great sense of urgency. When the first Christians spoke of a Kingdom to Come, they weren't talking of some event in the far distant future, but of something that was going to happen in the next few weeks – months at the most. They believed the end of the world was well and truly nigh. People became Christians because they were scared. Shit-scared. Also – wonderful simplicity. There were so many cults, so many different gods – Christianity swept all that away. One God – one road to salvation and life everlasting. But as Celsus said, it was nothing more than a very obvious variation on existing pagan myths, cleverly adapted to appeal to the naive and simple-minded. Celsus – Greek philosopher, second century. Poor bugger.

VIN Never heard of him.

KATE Neither have I.

ELEANOR Why "poor bugger"?

HUMPHREY When the Emperor Constantine made Christianity the official religion of the Rome Empire – when it became the Roman Church – all heretical voices, like Celsus, were well and truly silenced. My friend Bob wrote a book about him. Bob Hobbes. I helped with the research. Never found a publisher, everyone turned it down, arseholes. Celsus was shocked by the idea of a bodily resurrection; "revolting and impossible", he called it. Dead right. He may've been a heretic but he was no fool, old Celsus. Now that's an interesting word: "heresy". Comes from the Greek. *Hairesis* – "an act of choosing". Heresy means thinking for yourself. Orthodoxy means thinking what you're told to think. And since most people like to be told what to think, orthodoxy always wins. Almost always. So. Having made Christianity the Church of Rome, the odious Constantine and a group of bishops met at a place called Nicaea. 325 AD (sorry, CE). There they created the infrastructure of Christianity. They decided which old Jewish texts should constitute the Bible; they wrote the creed, invented the Trinity. Shortly thereafter the oh-so-Christian Constantine murdered his son and killed his wife by having her boiled alive in her bathwater. Slowly. He was later canonised by the Russian Orthodox Church. Make of that what you will.

ELEANOR   Is that true? – Constantine inventing the Trinity?

HUMPHREY   Absolutely. The Roman Church has been inventing itself for the past seventeen hundred years. The Assumption of the Virgin Mary, transubstantiation, the celibacy of priests – no basis in scripture for any of them. And it's still going on. The absurd idea of papal infallibility wasn't cooked up till 1870.

ELEANOR   You still haven't answered Kate's question.

HUMPHREY   Which was?

ELEANOR   Why it survived.

HUMPHREY   Haven't I? I thought I had. First of all, a sense of urgency. Save yourself while there's still time. Next, believe in Jesus and you'll float up to heaven and enjoy life everlasting. Then, because of the appalling Constantine, it became the religion of the state. Two great sources of power became one. It'd be amazing if it hadn't survived.

KATE   Religious faith is not a source of power.

HUMPHREY   I can't believe I heard you say that.

KATE   Not in the way you mean.

HUMPHREY Of course it is. Perhaps the most potent. "Don't ask for proof – just believe." Persuade people to believe what you can't prove and you have immense power. As long as people accept a religion that has no basis in logical argument or even common sense, they'll accept political control for the same reason (or lack of it). Dictators have known this throughout history. Look at Pius the Twelfth and Adolf Hitler. It's not surprising they got on so well together.

> [*A moment of silence. A night-bird calls amongst the shadows, prompting* CHARLES *to glance at the dark landscape.*]

CHARLES These people – the unseen people who are following you – if you are being followed – which seems to me doubtful – who are they?

HUMPHREY I don't know.

ELEANOR People from the clinic, I thought you said.

VIN Or the Vatican.

HUMPHREY Well, yes, either – both.

CHARLES Yes, but who exactly are you talking about? The police, the Swiss Guard, the Pope on a Lambretta?

HUMPHREY How can I convince you? This is no joke. They're dangerous men.

CHARLES *Who* are dangerous men?

HUMPHREY I don't know! I don't know! [*Brief pause.*] I don't know who they are. I don't know how they operate. But I know they exist. Mr Morandi was burnt to a cinder on the A6. John Paul the First was murdered in his bed. If they can poison a Pope, there'd be no problem getting rid of me – or indeed the whole lot of us, if they think it's necessary.

> [*A frisson of fear.*]

VIN   Are you talking about the Mafia?

HUMPHREY   Possibly. The Mafia – or P2 [*pronounced pay-duay*].

ELEANOR   Pay-duay...?

HUMPHREY   Pee-two. P for Propaganda. An illegal masonic lodge based in Rome.

CHARLES   An illegal masonic lodge...!

VIN   I've heard of P2. Right-wing extremists. Their ultimate aim is to re-establish fascism in Italy.

CHARLES   Oh please.

VIN   [*to* HUMPHREY] Isn't that right?

HUMPHREY   Yes, it is.

VIN   A man was killed in London.

HUMPHREY   Roberto Calvi.

VIN   Right. The papers were full of it. Banker. A member of P2.

HUMPHREY   Chairman of the Banco Ambrosiano. Friend of the Vatican.

VIN   They found him hanging underneath Waterloo Bridge.

HUMPHREY   Blackfriars.

VIN   Right. Blackfriars.

CHARLES   He killed himself.

HUMPHREY   That was the official verdict. In fact he was murdered by a Mafia thug called Francesco Di Carlo. Di Carlo was based in England. Imported cocaine and heroin. He strangled Calvi and strung him up under Blackfriars Bridge. Calvi's pockets were filled with stones: a coded message that this was a Mafia punishment killing.

CHARLES   What's all this got to do with the Vatican?

HUMPHREY Calvi had a close working relationship with Bishop Marcinkus, head of the Vatican Bank – or to give it its proper name – *L'Istituto per le Opere di Religione*. The Institute for Religious Works. Do me a favour. Tax evasion, traffic in stolen and forged securities, political bribery, laundering drug money for the Sicilian Mafia.

KATE The Vatican...?

HUMPHREY As Bishop Marcinkus once said, "You can't run the Church on Hail Marys."

VIN So why was Calvi murdered?

HUMPHREY He was being investigated for fraud. Huge sums of money were involved. Calvi had a nest-egg of four hundred million dollars. It's never been found. If he had lived and been brought to trial, he would've implicated the Vatican Bank – and the smallest question mark over the Vatican's integrity had to be eradicated at all costs.

CHARLES All this happened twenty years ago. A lot changes in twenty years.

HUMPHREY Does it? Catholicism claims to represent the Absolute Truth. Absolute Truth demands Absolute Power.

[*The sound of gunfire.* HUMPHREY *swings round, alarmed.*]

Are you sure they're poachers?

KATE That's what the farmer said.

[*Another shot.*]

HUMPHREY They're getting closer.

KATE They're down in the valley.

HUMPHREY No – much closer.

KATE Don't worry about it. We heard them last night.

VIN   And the night before.

> [*Another shot. A dog is barking in the valley.* HUMPHREY *tries to reassure himself.*]

HUMPHREY   Poachers. Yes. Well, let's hope you're right.

> [*The dog is still barking;* HUMPHREY's *nervousness gets the better of him; he yells into the darkness.*]

Shut up!

> [*The dog continues to bark.*]

Forgive me. I'm sorry.

VIN   [*hisses to* CHARLES] It's not right, keeping him here –

CHARLES   For God's sake leave all that to me.

VIN   – it's not right.

CHARLES   Stop it, Vin – don't make matters worse.

VIN   [*bristling*] What do you mean?

CHARLES   You know perfectly well –

VIN   Now look –

KATE   Vin, don't –

VIN   I've had enough – more than enough –

KATE   Vin!

VIN   [*to* CHARLES] You are not in charge! You are not the camp commandant! Suppose they're not poachers – suppose they're – killers, like he said – professional killers.

CHARLES   Don't talk nonsense. We've heard them every night.

VIN   We don't know they're the same people.

ELEANOR   That's right.

VIN   If they find him here, we're in real trouble – if he's not here, nobody can prove anything.

CHARLES If we take him to the police, we're doing the right thing – and that's what we're going to do.

VIN Why don't you stop giving orders?

CHARLES Somebody's got to make a decision.

VIN Why you?

HUMPHREY Stop this – please stop! Just let me go. You don't have to drive me anywhere. I'll walk. You'll never see me again. I promise.

[*He goes towards the door.* CHARLES *pushes him back.*]

CHARLES You know we can't do that.

ELEANOR Listen to him, Charles

CHARLES [*to* ELEANOR] He crashed his car just a few yards away. The police'll know he came here.

HUMPHREY You can say I ran away.

CHARLES Nobody's going to believe that.

ELEANOR They might.

CHARLES Eleanor, please. Be sensible. [*He turns to* HUMPHREY.] Now look. We are not going to lie to the police.

KATE [*to* HUMPHREY] And you couldn't walk all the way to Montivellara. It's much too far.

CHARLES You will stay here until morning and then we'll –

HUMPHREY Believe me, you're making a big mistake.

CHARLES Please don't interrupt.

HUMPHREY May I say one thing?

CHARLES No. In fact, if I were you I'd keep very quiet. The more you say, the more you make trouble for yourself.

[*Pause.* HUMPHREY *is silent.*]

You seem to take a strange delight in smashing ideas and beliefs that most people respect. And cherish.

Well, I've had enough of it. I will not be lectured by someone like you. You're a very destructive little man, Mr Biddulph. And you're wrong. Profoundly wrong. There are many things – we can't explain them but we know they happen. Most of us need these mysteries. We need to believe in them. You may not. I do. And I will not be told what to believe or not to believe by you or anyone.

[HUMPHREY *is silent.*]

Well, go on. Say something. React.

HUMPHREY What "mysteries" are you talking about?

CHARLES Well. For example. Near death experiences.

HUMPHREY What about them?

CHARLES You know what I'm talking about?

HUMPHREY I do.

CHARLES The sensation of travelling through a dark tunnel towards the light. The feeling of leaving the body. A sense of blissful well-being. All these things have been described again and again. They may not prove anything about death or an afterlife, but they do suggest very strongly that something extraordinary happens when we die, something more than just ceasing to exist.

KATE That's right.

CHARLES Hundreds of people have had the same experience – thousands. It's well documented. The same sensations.

[HUMPHREY *is silent.*]

So what do you say to that?

HUMPHREY Well, it's difficult to, uh...

CHARLES Difficult to what?

HUMPHREY I don't want to antagonise you even more.

CHARLES What do you mean?

[*Brief pause.*]

HUMPHREY It's oxygen starvation.

CHARLES What is...?

HUMPHREY The dying brain is starved of oxygen. This causes the neurons to rush about in an attempt to restore normalcy. This frenzied activity creates a sensation of light in the centre of our visual field, hence the light-at-the-end-of-the-tunnel effect; it also plays merry hell with the areas of the brain that deal with memory and emotion, hence the illusion that life is flashing before our eyes. At the same time, the brain releases opiate-like substances that create a feeling of euphoria – total bliss. Isn't that amazing?

KATE What about floating above the body?

HUMPHREY As we die we lose sensory awareness of our limbs and internal organs. The brain receives none of the usual sensory feedback and is thus detached from the physical body. Floating, as it were.

VIN So that's it? Nothing more than an automatic chain reaction. The body shutting itself down.

HUMPHREY Rather wonderful though, don't you think? Awesome. Infinitely more satisfying than all that quasi mystical mumbo-jumbo.

KATE Why do you hate it so much?

HUMPHREY Hate what?

KATE Faith. People believing.

HUMPHREY I don't hate it.

KATE Perhaps it frightens you.

HUMPHREY No, it irritates me.

KATE   Why? Belief can help people. It certainly doesn't do them any harm.

HUMPHREY   It's always harmful to peddle falsehood as truth.

KATE   We don't know it's false.

HUMPHREY   We don't know it's true.

KATE   Do you have to prove everything?

HUMPHREY   I try to, yes. I remember lying in bed one morning watching CNN. There was an item about the Hubble telescope; it'd been repaired or repositioned or something. And I thought how delightful it would be if, while gazing into the distant depths of outer space, the astronomers suddenly saw the heavenly host, all those cherubim and seraphim, flapping about like giant seagulls outside the gates of paradise. If God is all-powerful, why doesn't he arrange for something like that to happen? Then we'd all be believers.

KATE   Religion isn't about proving things. It's about faith.

HUMPHREY   I don't understand it, you see, that's the problem.

KATE   There's nothing to understand. Faith is.

HUMPHREY   Is what?

KATE   A gift. If you don't have it you can't understand it.

HUMPHREY   Why not?

KATE   That's impossible to answer.

HUMPHREY   Why?

KATE   Faith is intangible. If you could define it, it wouldn't be faith.

HUMPHREY   Here we go. The typically evasive response. You always gets fobbed off with that sort of reply: "The mysteries of God can never be understood by mere mortals." It's pure sophistry.

KATE   I can't define it because faith means something different to everyone.

HUMPHREY All right. What does it mean to you?

KATE To me...? I suppose it means I believe there's something beyond the world and my experience of the world – something that's unseen and unprovable – but nevertheless something that gives this known world an extra significance and meaning. Something that makes sense of everything. It's not a question of "how can I believe in God?" I simply can't disbelieve in him.

HUMPHREY Fine. Very good. Rather moving. But when I say I don't understand about faith, I don't mean I don't understand what faith is, I mean I don't understand why it is so valued. "A man (or woman) of faith," they say admiringly, as if it's some kind of virtue. Why? Why is it so highly regarded?

CHARLES You're talking nonsense, drivel, utter garbage.

[HUMPHREY *is in no mood to be interrupted.*]

HUMPHREY For instance. You're standing at the corner of a street. A man comes up – a stranger, a man you've never seen before – he comes up and offers you a brand new Rolls-Royce for five thousand pounds. Cash. The deal is this: you give him the cash in advance and you wait on the street corner until he appears with the car, which he promises to do very shortly. Do you have faith in this man and give him the five thousand pounds, or do you tell him to bugger off and find some other sucker?

KATE That's not what faith is about.

HUMPHREY Seems very like it to me.

KATE That's hope, not faith.

HUMPHREY "Unquestioning confidence" it says in the dictionary. Faith. Unquestioning confidence. Is that something to be admired? Is it? Not in my book it isn't. More like plain stupidity. If I had to choose a favourite disciple it'd be Thomas Didymus. The only one with a grain of common sense. The door opens – in walks Jesus. "I've died but here I am alive again." It seems a perfectly reasonable response to say "prove it". What happens? He gets ticked off. "Blessèd are they that have not seen and yet have believed." Why? Bollocks. What's so blessèd about unquestioning belief? It's like those people you see on the TV news. An entire family wiped out by a plane crash or terrorist bomb. The sole survivor – usually an overweight woman in her fifties – is shown putting cellophane-wrapped flowers on the site of the massacre. On comes the local priest or parson. "Her faith is stronger than ever." And we're expected to admire that. Why? *Why?* I hurl things at the TV screen. I can't bear to see their fatuous self-deluding faces.

KATE Why do you take it all so personally?

HUMPHREY It *is* personal, that's why. It's very personal. You're right. I do hate it. Faith diminishes the human race. It robs us of our reason. Replaces knowledge with superstition. Makes us abject unthinking slabs.

KATE You may think that, I do not.

HUMPHREY Well of course not, you're a believer.

KATE It's so easy to sneer.

HUMPHREY I wasn't sneering.

KATE Sounded like it to me.

HUMPHREY Sorry, not intended.

KATE Faith does not diminish the human race. It gives us spiritual stature. It allows us to be more than we think we are.

HUMPHREY Let me ask you a question, Mrs Coker. The brain works because neurons send each other little messages. Tiny electrical impulses. These points of contact are called synapses. Here's the question. If you were to count all these points of contact at the rate of one a second, how long would it take to count them all?

KATE How long...?

HUMPHREY How many hours, months or years would it take to count all the synapses in your brain?

KATE I've no idea.

HUMPHREY Guess.

KATE No idea at all.

HUMPHREY Guess.

KATE Well obviously a great many. Five hundred years.

HUMPHREY Mrs Minto?

ELEANOR A thousand.

HUMPHREY Any advance on a thousand?

VIN A million.

HUMPHREY The answer is thirty-two million. One a second for thirty-two million years. And yet, despite this astounding resource of intelligence and perception, people still insist on believing in astrology, in statues that weep, alien abduction, Our Lady of Lourdes, scientology, mystical stigmata and the whole wretched farrago of fairy tales and wishful thinking. There's a website for people who believe angels actually exist. They send e-mails to each other. "I saw an angel in the back yard last week." Ludicrous. The Mormons tell us that a heavenly spirit appeared to the Prophet Joseph Smith in upstate New York – gave him gold plates upon which were written the Wurdz o' Gahd. It's pure Monty Python. The Prophet Joseph Smith! Beyond parody. There was a Russian

Orthodox sect who thought self-castration was
the answer. They took a sharp knife and with a cry
of "Christ is risen!" cut off their cocks. This, they
believed, was their passport to eternal bliss. [*He mimes
the act.*] Christ is risen! And don't let's forget the
happy clappies: babbling like lunatics and pretend-
ing they're talking in tongues. Rational men and
women behaving like demented children. And
that, of course, is precisely what they *are* doing.
Christianity derives its strength from the delusional
fantasy of a never-ending childhood. God the Father,
Mary the Mother of God. We're all God's children.
It's just an anaesthetic. A way to avoid the painful
truths of human existence. Grow up! Grow up! For
Christ's sake, grow up!

CHARLES   All right, it may be a delusion. What's wrong with
that? I mean – if it helps people and gives them hope
– well, fine – why not? It's comforting.

HUMPHREY   Lots of things are comforting. Mars Bars are comforting, getting drunk is comforting, masturbation
is very comforting. God, if there is one, gave us the
power of reason. Let it not fust in us unused.

CHARLES   You're missing the point entirely. Religion is an attempt to create an ordered life. Forget all the dogma
and mysticism. Not important. Religion is the basis
for morality. Destroy religious belief and you're left
with moral anarchy.

HUMPHREY   I don't see why. Morality is a matter of individual
choice. Isn't that right? Proper respect for other
people. To leave all the decisions to some tut-tutting
all-powerful deity is an evasion of responsibility.

CHARLES   We need the structure. We need the discipline. Without some sort of moral framework, we'd be lost, no
better than animals.

HUMPHREY But we are animals.

CHARLES Exactly! That's what I'm saying. And that's why religion is so important. Creating order out of chaos. That's what it's all about.

HUMPHREY I'll tell you what's it all about. Happy endings. Isn't that what everyone wants? Isn't that the ultimate appeal of all religions? Something better to come. That's what they're selling. The hope of a bright new happiness beyond the nursing home days. A land with no arthritis, no dementia and none of the other humiliations of old age. Whenever I can I visit my mother in Godalming, at the Orchard Bank Residential Home. The old people sit in identical rooms, identically furnished, with a few scraps of personal memorabilia. First thing in the morning, the nurses go from room to room and switch on the television. "It's company," they say, "it keeps the old dears happy." My mother has to wear continence knickers, poor old thing. They have a brand name. Conti-Nix. N-I-X. My mother's ninety-three. She's lost her memory. Completely. She's also gone blind. But she can't remember she's gone blind. She sits in her chair all day, listening for approaching footsteps. You can hear her voice as you walk along the corridor: "Would you switch the light on please?" – "Would you switch the light on please?" – "Would you switch the light on please?"

[*There is a moment of silence before* KATE *speaks.*]

KATE Doesn't it frighten you?

HUMPHREY What?

KATE Nothingness. Emptiness. Oblivion.

HUMPHREY We don't worry about what happened before we were born. Why should we worry about what happens after we die?

[*Pause.*]

VIN   You may be right about happy endings. People see life as a narrative, wouldn't you say? A beginning, a middle and a satisfactory explanation at the end. "What's the meaning of it all?" my old mum used to say, "what are we here for?" She liked religion for the same reason she liked Agatha Christie. All loose ends tied up in the last chapter. A nice happy ending.

[ELEANOR *springs to her feet.*]

ELEANOR   Ssshhh!

KATE   What is it?

ELEANOR   There's somebody out there.

KATE   What? Where?

[ELEANOR *points at the shadowy landscape beyond the terrace.*]

ELEANOR   Out there. By the pool.

[*They all listen.*]

KATE   I can't hear anything.

CHARLES   Neither can I.

[*They all peer into the darkness.*]

VIN   Can't see anyone.

ELEANOR   Somebody's moving about.

CHARLES   Might be an animal.

KATE   Or one of the poachers.

[VIN *takes a step towards the edge of the terrace and calls (rather cautiously).*]

VIN   Hullo! Hullo!

[*Silence.*]

Who's there? *Chi è?*

[*Silence. He turns to* ELEANOR.]

Nothing. Nobody.

ELEANOR   Somebody was there. [*to* KATE] Didn't you hear it?

KATE   Well, no.

CHARLES   Hear what?

ELEANOR   Somebody moving about in the bushes.

CHARLES   Kate's right. Probably one of the poachers.

ELEANOR   It might be those people... Looking for him.

CHARLES   Most unlikely.

ELEANOR   Why?

VIN   Nobody's going to come looking for anyone in the middle of the night.

ELEANOR   Why not?

VIN   They'll wait till morning.

ELEANOR   How do you know that? They have special lights. Infra-red or something – they can see in the dark.

CHARLES   There's nothing to worry about.

ELEANOR   They're dangerous men, Charles! Didn't you hear what he said? They're killers!

CHARLES   Calm down, calm down. Nothing to worry about.

ELEANOR   Do stop saying that. [*She turns to* HUMPHREY.] This is all your fault.

HUMPHREY   I'm sorry...?

ELEANOR   It scares me. What you said.

HUMPHREY   I'm sorry. I had no intention of, uh...

ELEANOR   It made me think about things I don't want to think about.

VIN   Like what?

ELEANOR   All sorts of things.

[*Silence. Everyone is looking at her.*]

Alice.

CHARLES   Alice...?

KATE   What about her?

ELEANOR   I thought of Alice living alone. Being unhappy.

CHARLES   She's not unhappy.

ELEANOR   How do you know?

CHARLES   Please stop this.

ELEANOR   We never talk about it, never.

CHARLES   There's nothing to talk about.

ELEANOR   [*to* KATE] We were in a hotel. Near Oxford. Somehow we managed to get away for the weekend. "Leave her," I said – I can hear myself saying it – "let's make a life together. Leave her!"

CHARLES   She is not unhappy.

ELEANOR   How do you know? You don't even think about her.

CHARLES   Of course I do.

ELEANOR   That's the way you cope.

CHARLES   Eleanor, please...

ELEANOR   Ignore all the unpleasant things. Pretend they don't exist.

CHARLES   Well – what's wrong with that?

ELEANOR   Everything. It's not the truth.

CHARLES   It avoids pain.

ELEANOR   Is that so very important?

CHARLES   It is to me.

ELEANOR   [*to* KATE] Is she unhappy?

KATE   I don't know.

ELEANOR   Yes, you do. You see her. You have lunch together.

CHARLES   [*surprised, to* KATE] Do you?

KATE   She's my friend, Charles.

ELEANOR   She's unhappy and I shall pay for it. [*to* HUMPHREY] I don't care whether you can prove it or not, I know there's something, some sort of presence, watching over us, watching us day and night, someone who sees everything we do, who knows our deepest secrets, and who, one day, will bring us to a final judgement. I'm sure of that. I *know* it.

[*Silence.*]

VIN   Perhaps Charles is right. About avoiding pain. I do it all the time. I'm not as brave as Eleanor. Anything upsetting. Turn away. And why not? Life would be intolerable if we didn't have a few illusions to hide behind. All this searching for the truth – a bit over-rated, if you ask me. The truth becomes unavoidable soon enough. Why go looking for it? Too bloody pain-ful.

KATE   Oh Vin.

VIN   Oh Vin what?

KATE   Why do you have to be so cynical?

VIN   Is that being cynical? I don't think it is. None of this can be proved, after all – so what's the point? There is no such thing as The Truth capital T. It's all a question of personal preference. You like to believe. He prefers not to. You pays your money and you takes your choice.

KATE   Human beings *need* to believe. We're spiritual crea-tures as well as physical.

HUMPHREY   Spirituality does not require belief.

KATE   Believing is part of our nature.

HUMPHREY   Not of mine.

KATE   Have you never –in the whole of your life –have you never believed in anything?

HUMPHREY   Well of course I have. When I was a child I believed
in everything. Father Christmas, God, Andy Pandy.
Then my father died. He was taken ill on my eighth
birthday. The doctor didn't know what it was. The
pain got worse. My father was convinced it was
cancer. An appointment was made with a doctor in
Harley Street. My mother went with him. They were
planning to catch a lunchtime train to London. I
happened to be standing in the hall when they left.
It was the last time I ever saw him. As the train
approached, my father jumped in front of it. Killed
instantly. I couldn't accept the fact that he'd disap-
peared out of my life for ever. "Dad! Where are you?
Come back!" A post mortem showed he'd died un-
necessarily. There was no sign of cancer. My mother
consulted a medium. A spiritualist. I found it all
rather creepy. One day she came home in a state of
high excitement. My dad had apparently "come
through" and told her he was delighted with the new
lino on the kitchen floor. My mother thought this
was conclusive proof that his soul or whatever had
survived the ravages of the 1:32 to Charing Cross.
"But Mum," I said, "we haven't got new lino in the
kitchen." "Not yet, no," she said, "but I'm thinking
of getting some." She was totally convinced. I, on the
other hand, chose to cope with my father's death by
trying to live without illusions. From that moment
on, everything changed. I resolved to take nothing
on trust. To demand absolute proof.

KATE   That's not the answer.

HUMPHREY   Why not?

KATE   If you demand proof, you're ignoring the possibility
of something bigger, more extraordinary, more
astonishing, than we can ever possibly imagine.

HUMPHREY We were told at school that the earth travelled round the sun at sixty-six thousand, six hundred miles an hour. What could be more extraordinary, more astonishing than that? I lay in the back garden and stared up at the sky. It was the summer after Dad killed himself. I tried to feel the motion of the earth. The sensation of spinning through the universe at this colossal speed. Of course, I felt nothing. But I became completely obsessed by this notion. I thought of it day and night. And then one morning, as I was waking up, I suddenly felt it. The lurching onward motion of the earth as it hurtled round the sun. I remember clinging to the bed, terrified I'd be thrown off and find myself spinning hopelessly through space, for ever and ever amen. Everywhere I went I would hang on to walls or floors or park railings. I began to feel it all the time: this great surging forward thrust. I couldn't understand why no one else could feel it. Things became increasingly difficult. I strapped myself to the bed and refused to move. My mother took me to a specialist at Guy's Hospital. The treatment took several months, but eventually I was cured. But cured of what? It's happening now, don't forget, at this moment – as we sit here, as we speak, this second. Sixty-six thousand, six hundred miles an hour. Extraordinary! Astonishing! And because I tried – in my school-boyish way – to find absolute proof. I actually felt it. For those few days, those few weeks, I actually felt the great power of cosmic creation.

    [*Silence. The telephone rings. A moment of general astonishment.*]

KATE My God! The phone!

ELEANOR I'll get it...

> [*She runs to the house and grabs the phone, which is on a table beside the french windows.*]

Hullo, *pronto?* – Lucy! Hang on a minute. [*to* KATE] It's Lucy.

> [KATE *takes the phone.*]

KATE Lucy. Is everything all right? – Oh good – Yes, yes, we're fine. The phone's been cut off. There was a storm and it did something to the phone – Yes, I know we should've brought the mobile – How are you, Lucy? – Oh good – Oh good – Good, I'm so pleased – Yes, Saturday. We'll be home about seven.

VIN Eight.

KATE Maybe a bit later – Yes, all right – We will – Take care of yourself, darling. Much love from us all. Bye, darling, bye.

> [KATE *hangs up.*]

VIN Is she all right?

KATE She was worried to death – she's been trying to get through for a couple of days.

VIN Bloody Italians. You'd think they'd let us know the phone was back on.

> [*The phone call has restored a sense of the outside world. Everyone struggles to regain the comfort of normality.*]

CHARLES [*to* KATE] But she's all right?

KATE Oh yes, she's fine.

ELEANOR What time's the flight on Saturday?

KATE Three forty-five.

CHARLES We'll have to check in about two.

VIN That means leaving here when?

KATE Ten-ish.

VIN   No later.

CHARLES   We can go straight down the A1. It shouldn't take too long.

VIN   I hate that road. All those lunatics doing ninety miles an hour. Minimum.

KATE   It's better than the coast road.

VIN   Is it?

ELEANOR   That'd take hours.

CHARLES   Let me suggest a compromise. We'll drive across to Orvieto and pick up the A1 from there. How about that?

KATE   Fine.

CHARLES   [*to* VIN] All right for you?

VIN   Whatever you say.

CHARLES   Good, good. Excellent.

HUMPHREY   What about me?

[*They all stare at* HUMPHREY.]

CHARLES   You...?

HUMPHREY   What's going to happen to me?

CHARLES   We'll take you to Montivellara. First thing in the morning. Take you to the police.

[VIN *tries to interrupt, but to no avail.*]

VIN   Just a minute –

CHARLES   It'll all take some time, no doubt, so we'll need to make an early start.

HUMPHREY   [*appalled*] But you can't do this. You mustn't! Haven't you heard what I've been saying? The police'll send me straight back to Rome.

CHARLES   That has nothing to do with us.

HUMPHREY   These people are above the law, they're ruthless!

CHARLES   In that case, do something about it.

HUMPHREY   All right. What do you suggest?

CHARLES   Talk to Father Henriques. Promise to keep quiet. Meet them halfway.

HUMPHREY   I can't do that!

CHARLES   Why not?

HUMPHREY   I told you, for Christ's sake!

CHARLES   Then you've only yourself to blame.

> [HUMPHREY *blazes with anger.*]

HUMPHREY   Listen! I spent most of my days in the clinic in a state of boiling rage. They were keeping me a prisoner! – as they'd kept mankind a prisoner for the last two thousand years! There was a crucifix above my bed. It focused my feelings in a wonderfully liberating way. I screamed abuse at that mournful totem. And then one day my self-control snapped. I tore the crucifix from the wall and smashed it across my knee. The figure of Christ flew off and skidded across the floor like a drunken Barbie doll. I picked it up and ripped it apart, plastic limb from plastic limb. There was nothing left. Nothing left. Nothing. [*Brief pause.*] How can I possibly "meet them halfway"?

> [CHARLES *is profoundly shocked by this. He stares at* HUMPHREY.]

CHARLES   All right. Fine. If that's what you want, take the car. Take it.

VIN   What?

CHARLES   Take the car.

VIN   Yes, take it!

CHARLES   We'll ring the police in the morning. Say it's been stolen. That should give you enough time.

HUMPHREY Are you sure...?

CHARLES I want you out of here – out!

ELEANOR [*to* CHARLES] You should've done this hours ago.

VIN We told you.

CHARLES Never mind, we're doing it now.

KATE [*to* HUMPHREY] Are you all right to drive?

HUMPHREY All right? How do you mean?

KATE You've had a lot to drink.

HUMPHREY I'll be fine.

KATE Shall I make some coffee?

CHARLES I think he should go now. In case he's being followed. He should go before they catch up with him.

HUMPHREY You're right. Absolutely.

CHARLES Where are the car keys?

VIN Here...

[*He gives them to* HUMPHREY.]

HUMPHREY Thanks. I'll need a road map – do you have a road map I could borrow...?

CHARLES In the car.

ELEANOR No, upstairs. You were checking the route.

CHARLES Ah yes...

[CHARLES *goes towards the house.*]

HUMPHREY There is one thing. I hate to ask.

CHARLES What's that?

HUMPHREY I feel terribly conspicuous in these pyjamas.

CHARLES I'll see what I can find.

HUMPHREY Thank you.

[CHARLES *exits into the house. Silence.*]

Well. What can I say? I'm deeply grateful.

ELEANOR Well, good luck.

KATE Yes. Good luck.

VIN *Buona fortuna!*

KATE Are you sure you'll be all right?

HUMPHREY I feel like the man in the story. He was climbing a mountain. All by himself, halfway up an Alp or some equally perilous peak. A sheer drop of many thousands of feet to the valley far below. Suddenly the tiny ledge on which he's standing crumbles and gives way. He's left clinging on by his fingertips. He's not a religious man, but, like so many of us in extremis, he decides that God is his only chance of salvation. He looks up at the sky and says, "If there's anyone up there, please save me." To his amazement, a great voice echoes through the clouds: "Have faith. Let go. Have faith and I will save you." The man stares up at the sky. He considers this proposition for a moment, and then says, "Is there anyone else up there?"

> [CHARLES *returns with a road map, an old sweater and a pair of chinos.*]

CHARLES Here...

HUMPHREY Thank you. Thank you very much. [*He takes off his bomber jacket and dumps it on a chair.*] I should get to Bob's by the morning, don't you think? Easily. Bob Hobbes. I'll phone the police straight away. Tell them your car's been stolen.

CHARLES We'll do that.

HUMPHREY Will you? Fine.

KATE Then what?

> [HUMPHREY *is putting on the sweater and chinos.*]

HUMPHREY Well, that rather depends, doesn't it? I mean, you know, on what happens. With my pursuers, and so on. [*to* CHARLES] Give me your address and I'll post this back to you.

CHARLES   Don't bother.

HUMPHREY   Very kind. So generous. Thank you.

KATE   What about money? Do you have any money?

HUMPHREY   Well, no...

KATE   Give him some money, Vin.

VIN   [*taking out his wallet*] How much do you need?

HUMPHREY   Well just, perhaps – [*He takes some banknotes.*] – this should be more than enough. Thank you very much. [*He smiles his thanks to everyone.*] It's been – actually – a pleasure to meet you all.

[CHARLES *offers the gun to* HUMPHREY.]

CHARLES   You'd better take this.

[HUMPHREY *hesitates.*]

We don't want it.

HUMPHREY   All right. Whatever you say. [*He takes the gun.*] Thank you.

[*He exits quickly. Everyone heaves a sigh of relief.*]

ELEANOR   Thank God. Thank God he's gone.

VIN   [*to* CHARLES] Well done. Smart move.

CHARLES   What was?

VIN   Letting him take the car.

CHARLES   Your idea, old cock, not mine.

VIN   Well, whatever. It was the right thing to do.

ELEANOR   I'm glad you gave him the gun.

CHARLES   We don't want it here, do we?

VIN   We certainly do not.

KATE   I wonder if he was telling the truth...

CHARLES   Well of course not. Total nonsense from start to finish.

VIN   You think so?

CHARLES   Don't you? Dear God, am I the only sane one here?

KATE   Why should he make it up?

CHARLES   Because he's barking mad. All that stuff about falling off the world. Breaking the crucifix. Not exactly the voice of sanity.

[*A car is heard driving away.*]

VIN   Well. There he goes. [*Pause.*] Dear Auntie Lil. Having a lovely time. Weather perfect. Met a nice man who says Jesus Christ is a fake. Talk about laugh. Wish you were here. Love Vinnie.

[*Nobody laughs.*]

CHARLES   We ought to make a plan.

VIN   A plan?

CHARLES   We'll tell the police he forced us to do it. To give him the car. At gunpoint. If we're asked.

VIN   Which he did. In a way.

CHARLES   The same with my clothes.

VIN   All right.

CHARLES   Don't say I offered...

VIN   No, no.

ELEANOR   We should all stick to the same story. No mention of Mr Morandi and the letter. He came here, pulled out a gun, and forced us to give him the car.

CHARLES   Right. Agreed?

KATE   All right.

CHARLES   No point in making things difficult for ourselves.

KATE   No, no, you're right.

[VIN *has picked up* HUMPHREY'*s bomber jacket.*]

CHARLES What are you doing?

[VIN *is searching through the pockets.*]

VIN Having a look at his things. [*He opens the wallet.*] Family photographs, driving licence, Visa card in the name of Roberto Bartolini.

ELEANOR Who's Roberto Bartolini?

VIN The central heating engineer, presumably.

[*In another pocket he finds a folded piece of paper.*]

What's this?

[CHARLES *looks at it.*]

CHARLES Plans of a central heating system.

ELEANOR So he *was* telling the truth.

[CHARLES *prefers to sidestep this disturbing possibility.*]

CHARLES Not necessarily.

[*A strange whirring, thudding noise is heard, distant at first but drawing closer.*]

ELEANOR What's that?

CHARLES Sounds like a tractor.

ELEANOR Can't be.

[VIN *goes to the edge of the terrace.*]

VIN It's a helicopter!

[*The helicopter noise becomes increasingly loud.*]

CHARLES Turn the lights off! – turn the bloody lights off!

[VIN *runs to the house and turns off the lights. Everyone huddles together in the shadows. A powerful beam of light sweeps over the country-*

[*side and then across the terrace. By this time, the noise is deafening.*]

[*The helicopter moves away. The beam of light can no longer be seen. The engine noise gradually recedes.*]

VIN They're looking for him.

ELEANOR They'll see the car.

KATE Perhaps he'll find somewhere to hide.

ELEANOR I mean his car. The one he crashed.

VIN That means – they'll know he came here.

CHARLES They may not see it.

KATE Perhaps they're looking for something else.

VIN Like what?

ELEANOR Let's get out of here.

KATE And go where?

ELEANOR Anywhere – doesn't matter.

CHARLES How can we? He's got the car. There's nothing we can do.

[*The helicopter is returning.*]

KATE Lighten our darkness, we beseech thee, O Lord; and by thy great mercy defend us from all perils and dangers of this night; for the love of thy only Son, our Saviour Jesus Christ. Amen.

[*Her voice is drowned by the thudding roar of the helicopter's engine.*]

CURTAIN

FURTHER READING

Allegro, J.M. *The Dead Sea Scrolls* (Penguin, 1956)

Baigent, Michael, Leigh, Richard & Lincoln, Henry *The Holy Blood and the Holy Grail* (Cape, 1982)

Baigent, Michael & Leigh, Richard *The Dead Sea Scrolls Deception* (Cape, 1991)

Camus, Albert *The Myth of Sisyphus* (Hamish Hamilton, 1955)

Cornwell, John *A Thief in the Night* (Viking, 1989)

Cornwell, John *Hitler's Pope* (Viking, 1999)

Crossan, John Dominic *The Birth of Christianity* (HarperSanFrancisco, 1999)

Cupitt, Don *After God* (Weidenfeld & Nicolson, 1997)

Davis, Stephen T. (editor) *The Resurrection* (OUP, 1997)

Dodds, E.R. *The Greeks and the Irrational* (University of California Press, 1951)

Dodds, E.R. *Pagan and Christian in an Age of Anxiety* (Cambridge University Press, 1965)

Edelman, Gerald *Bright Air, Brilliant Fire* (BasicBooks, 1992)

Engelstein, Laura *Castration and the Heavenly Kingdom* (Cornell University Press, 1999)

Frazer, J.G. *The Golden Bough* (Macmillan, 1922)

Freke, Timothy & Gandy, Peter *The Jesus Mysteries* (Thorsons, 1999)

Fuller, Peter *Images of God* (Chatto & Windus, 1985)

Golb, Norman *Who wrote the Dead Sea Scrolls?* (Scribner, 1995)

Hebblethwaite, Peter *In the Vatican* (Sidgwick & Jackson, 1986)

Hitchens, Christopher *The Missionary Position* (Verso, 1995)

Hume, David *The Natural History of Religion* (OUP, 1993 reprint)

Humphrey, Nicholas *Soul Searching* (Chatto & Windus, 1995)

James, William *The Will to Believe* (Longman, Green and Co., 1897)

James, William *The Varieties of Religious Experience* (Longman, Green and Co., 1902)

Kennedy, Ludovic *All in the Mind* (Hodder & Stoughton, 1999)

Kersten, Holger & Gruber, Elmar R. *The Jesus Conspiracy* (Element, 1994)

Lockhart, Douglas *Jesus the Heretic* (Element, 1997)

Mackay, Charles *Extraordinary Popular Delusions and the Madness of Crowds* (Wordsworth, 1995 reprint)

O'Grady, Joan *Heresy* (Element, 1985).

Polkinghorne, John *Science and Creation* (SPCK, 1988)

Raw, Charles *The Money Changers* (Harvill, 1992)

Reade, Winwood *The Martyrdom of Man* (Cape, 1927 reprint)

Renan, Ernest *The Life of Jesus* (Watts & Co., 1935 reprint)

Reese, Thomas J. *Inside the Vatican* (Harvard University Press, 1998)

Shermer, Michael *Why People Believe Weird Things* (Freeman, 1997)

Smith, Morton *Jesus the Magician* (Gollancz, 1978).

Steiner, George *Real Presences* (Faber & Faber, 1989)

Storr, Anthony *Feet of Clay* (HarperCollins, 1996)

Stourton, Edward *Absolute Truth* (Viking, 1998)

Thompson, Thomas L. *The Bible in History* (Cape, 1999)

Todd, Olivier *Albert Camus: A Life* (Chatto & Windus 1997)

Tully, Mark *Lives of Jesus* (Penguin, 1996)

Von Franz, Marie-Louise *Creation Myths* (Spring Publications, 1972)

Warner, Marina *Alone of All Her Sex* (Weidenfeld & Nicolson, 1976)

Wills, Garry *Papal Sin* (Doubleday, 2000)

Wilson, A.N. *Jesus* (Sinclair-Stevenson, 1992)

Wilson, A.N. *God's Funeral* (John Murray, 1999)

Wroe, Ann *Pilate* (Cape, 1999)

Yallop, David *In God's Name* (Cape, 1984)